LET GOD CHANGE YOUR LIFE

LET GOD CHANGE YOUR LIFE

HOW TO KNOW AND FOLLOW JESUS

GREG LAURIE

David C Cook®

transforming lives together

LET GOD CHANGE YOUR LIFE
Published by David C Cook
4050 Lee Vance View
Colorado Springs, CO 80918 U.S.A.

David C Cook Distribution Canada
55 Woodslee Avenue, Paris, Ontario, Canada N3L 3E5

David C Cook U.K., Kingsway Communications
Eastbourne, East Sussex BN23 6NT, England

David C Cook and the graphic circle C logo
are registered trademarks of Cook Communications Ministries.

The website addresses recommended throughout this book are offered as a
resource to you. These websites are not intended in any way to be or imply an
endorsement on the part of David C Cook, nor do we vouch for their content.

See Bible-resource credits at the back of this book.
The author has added italics to Scripture quotations for emphasis.

LCCN 2010941778
ISBN 978-1-4347-0207-4
eISBN 978-1-4347-0368-2

© 2011 Greg Laurie
Published in association with the literary agency of FM Management,
24981 Dana Point Harbor Drive, Suite 110, Dana Point, CA 92629.

Portions of this book were previously published by
Kerygma Publishing, © Greg Laurie
How to Know God in 2006, ISBN 978-0-9777103-1-7
Making God Known in 2007, ISBN 978-0-9777103-6-2
Discipleship: The Road Less Taken in 2009, ISBN 978-0-9801831-6-0

Portions of this book were also previously published by Harvest House Publishers as
Discipleship: Giving God Your Best in 1993 © Greg Laurie, ISBN 978-1-56507-039-4

The Team: Alex Field, Sarah Schultz, Renada Arens, and Karen Athen
Cover Design: Amy Kiechlin
Cover Photo: iStock

Printed in the United States of America

First Edition 2011

1 2 3 4 5 6 7 8 9 10

021011

To Jonathan Allen Laurie,
a growing disciple of Jesus Christ
of whom I am very proud

Contents

INTRODUCTION

It has been said there are two things that are true of every person: *We all want to be happy,* and *we are all going to die.*

From the moment you and I were born, we have been on a quest. What we've been searching for hasn't always been clear, but we all want our lives to have meaning and purpose. And we want to be happy.

For me, this search began at a very early age. I was born into a chaotic environment. My mother, an alcoholic, married and divorced seven times. I had to grow up fast and learn how to take care of myself. And as I observed the adult world into which I had been immersed, as I watched all the drinking and partying, I thought to myself, *I don't want to live that way.* But by the time I was in high school, I was out drinking and partying with the best of them.

Then the 1960s drug revolution emerged on the scene. Rock stars such as Jimi Hendrix, Janis Joplin, and Jim Morrison told us to expand our minds through drug use. I had been told that if I took drugs, I would become "more aware." I definitely wanted to be more aware, so I started taking drugs, and I became more aware all right—*aware of how miserable I felt.*

Eventually, I went from smoking pot to taking LSD. But as our rock icons died one by one (Jimi Hendrix, Janis Joplin, and Jim Morrison all died, ironically, at the age of twenty-seven), I knew this was not the life I wanted to live.

I narrowed my search through the process of elimination. I knew what I sought wasn't in partying. And I didn't find it in drinking, affluence, or drugs. As far as I could tell, it wasn't in the adult world I had observed.

Then one day on my high school campus, I saw a really cute girl. A friend of mine was talking to her, so I walked up to them and waited for a chance to introduce myself. As I stood there, I noticed that in addition to a textbook and a notebook, she was carrying an unusual-looking book with a black leather cover and gold pages. I thought, *Oh, no! That's a Bible. This girl is a Jesus freak. What a waste of a perfectly cute girl!* I thought Christians were all a bit crazy. Something wasn't right about them. Why would anyone come to school carrying a Bible and talking about God as though He were her next-door neighbor? Don't get me wrong—*I believed in Jesus.* I had seen all His movies, and what I knew about Him (which wasn't much), I liked. When I was in trouble, I always called on Jesus. He was my God of choice in a crisis. But I never realized that Jesus could be *known* in a personal way.

One day at lunchtime, I was walking across campus and noticed the Christians out on the front lawn, singing songs about God. I sat down a few feet away, close enough to eavesdrop on their conversation (because the cute girl was there), but not close enough for my friends to assume that I was actually one of them, which would have been social suicide. As I listened and watched them sing songs about

God, I thought, *Look at these crazy people … they are so weird … they are so demented … and they are so … happy!*

Then I tried a new thought on for size: What if the Christians are right? What if God can be known in a personal way?

Then a youth pastor named Lonnie got up and spoke. I don't remember most of what he said, but I do remember one statement that hit me like a lightning bolt. He told the group, "Jesus said, 'You are either for Me or against Me.'" I thought, *Well, these Christians are definitely for Him. And I am not one of them. Does that mean that I am against Him?*

He continued, "If you want to give your life to Jesus right now and be forgiven of your sin, I want you to get up and walk forward, and I am going to lead you in a prayer." *There is no way I could do that,* I thought. *I would like to know God. I would like to have happiness and peace. But this won't work for me. I am not the religious type. I am too cynical, too mad at the world.*

Amazingly, I got up anyway, went forward, and prayed along with a handful of kids who did the same. It was as if time stood still as I called out to God, "Forgive me of my sin; come into my life."

I remember that as I finished praying, it felt like someone lifted a big load off my shoulders. And indeed it was lifted. The burden of sin and guilt I had been carrying for the first seventeen years of my life had been removed.

Then the school bell rang. Back to class!

But before I left, that really cute girl came up, hugged me, and said, "God bless you, brother." I thought, *This is good being a Christian!* But she and I never became more than friends. Or as my new Christian friends would say, she was "a sister in the Lord."

But God used her to get my attention. As I began to meet other Christians and grow in my newfound faith, I discovered what God was *really* like. I learned what it meant to have a personal relationship with Jesus Christ.

Many people today hold on to preconceived notions about God. Some envision God as an angry, hostile, and uptight Supreme Being who is in a perpetual bad mood and waiting to nail them when they sin. Others may think God is strange, because they have known strange people who call themselves Christians. Yet let's not blame their weirdness on Christianity. They were probably that way in the first place.

So what is God like? How does He look at us? And more importantly, does He approve or disapprove of us?

We find the answers in the pages of Scripture, where God reveals Himself. Jesus gives us a snapshot of God in the parable of the prodigal son. I think it could be more appropriately called the parable of the loving father, because Jesus portrays God as a heavenly Father who deeply loves us and desperately misses us when we go astray.

It is the story of a boy living at home with his dad and brother, who thinks to himself, *I'm sick and tired of living here. I'm tired of my father's rules. I'm tired of the regulations. I want to go out and live the life that I have chosen to live.* The bright lights of the big city called to him. So he went to his dad and said, "Give me the portion of the inheritance that is coming to me. I don't want to wait until you die. I want to experience life now."

The father gave his son what he asked for, and off the boy went. When he rolled into town, I am sure he was one popular guy … that is, until his money ran out. Lacking money and friends, he ended up hanging out with a bunch of pigs. *Literally.* What began as an adventure living high on the hog ended up a nightmare hanging out with hogs. Eventually, even their food started to look good to the young man.

Then it dawned on him how ridiculous his life had become. He decided it was time to go back to his father. Suddenly the home that he couldn't get away from fast enough, the home full of rules and regulations, looked much better. So he started his journey back.

While he was still a long way off, his father saw him. His father didn't turn away, but rather, started joyfully running toward the young man.

His father could have stopped short and said, "Whoa! Go take a bath, son! Then maybe I will give you a hug."

But that didn't happen. The young man's father embraced him and accepted him just as he was.

Still, there is something else to think about in this story.

In that culture, it was considered undignified for an older man to run. It just wasn't done. But the father knew that he had to get to his son as quickly as possible. Why? This son had dragged his family name through the mud. This son had spent his money on parties and prostitutes. The father knew that if he could get to his son and throw his arms around him, his boy would be safe.

So the father pulled his robe above his knees and sprinted toward his son, undignified though it was. Then he threw his arms around him and kissed him. The word used for "kissed" in this story could be better translated "smothered him with kisses."

However, he didn't leave his son the way he was. He told his servants, "Bring out the best robe and put it on him, and put a ring on his hand and sandals on his feet. And bring the fatted calf here and kill it, and let us eat and be merry; for this my son was dead and is alive again; he was lost and is found" (Luke 15:22–24).

Like the prodigal's father, God accepts us as we are. But He doesn't want to leave us that way. *God will change us.*

That day on my high school campus, as I eavesdropped on the Christians' meeting, I knew there was a God out there. And when I heard that God could come and live inside me, give me meaning and purpose, remove my guilt, and bring me to heaven when I die, it was an offer I couldn't refuse.

Many years have passed since then, yet I haven't once regretted my decision to respond to the invitation that day. Jesus Christ brought meaning and purpose to my life. He gave me a life worth living. Through the incredible privilege of pointing others to Jesus Christ over the years, I have seen Him do the same for them—time and time again.

The good news of Jesus Christ is as relevant today as it was when I responded, and these are critical times for sharing the message. There are doors open today that may not necessarily stay open forever. Speaking to the church of the last days, Jesus said, "See, I have set before you an open door, and no one can shut it" (Rev. 3:8). And speaking to His disciples, He said, "I tell you, open your eyes and look at the fields! They are ripe for harvest" (John 4:35 NIV).

You might be thinking, *Amen! I pray that the Lord will raise up more people to go out and share the good news.* But no one can honestly pray that this work will be done who is not actually willing to help do the work. Granted, not all of us are pastors, evangelists, or missionaries, but *all* of us are called to sow seeds. Everyone has a part to play. That means you. That means me. Unbelievers are not the enemy—they are people for whom Christ died. We need to remember we were each one of them once.

Are you a laborer in the harvest? The complainers are many. The observers are many. The spectators are many. The critics are many. But the laborers are few. We need laborers in the harvest. Will you become one?

In this book, I want to share about three critical parts of the Christian life: *How to Know God, Discipleship,* and *Making Him Known.* The purpose of this book is to call us back to radical New Testament Christian living: to know God, embrace discipleship, and share our faith in all its facets as Jesus taught us, and as the disciples and the early church lived it out.

In a biblical sense, radical Christian living is really normal Christian living. The first-century believers who followed Jesus Christ were men and women who turned their worlds upside down to follow the Messiah. And they lived the Christian life as Jesus presented it to them personally.

The good news is that we too can participate in this lifestyle.

What we often perceive as the Christian life is, in many ways, not what the Bible teaches. We need to ask ourselves whether we are living the Christian life as Jesus meant for us to live it. Is your life challenging? Exciting? Does it have purpose and direction? Or, do you find yourself depressed and afraid? If your Christian experience is dull, unfulfilling, or boring, then it's time to seriously examine the statements of Jesus concerning how to follow Him.

Ray Stedman said, "The chief mark of the Christian ought to be the absence of fear and the presence of joy. We have often quoted the description of a Christian as one who is completely fearless, continually cheerful, and constantly in trouble. It is that presence of joy and absence of fear that marks our genuine Christianity and proves that we really are what we claim to be."[1]

That is what the world needs more of today: *Christians who are full of joy and completely fearless.* After all, how can we expect to fulfill the Great Commission to go into all the world and make disciples if we don't even know what it is to be a disciple ourselves? As the saying goes, it takes one to make one.

Make no mistake about it: If you live this Christian life as Jesus taught it and as the early church lived it, you will enjoy life to its fullest as you walk in the center of the perfect will of God.

Join me in this spiritual odyssey as we follow the words of Jesus concerning knowing God, following Him, and telling others about Him. As we go through these steps as laid out by Jesus, it is my prayer that you will seriously consider them and apply them to your life.

If you do, the world may never be the same.

PART ONE

HOW TO KNOW GOD

1

GOD'S CURE FOR
HEART TROUBLE

Have you ever felt so stressed out that it seemed like everything was going wrong—all at once? Then, when it seemed like things couldn't get any worse, they did? Or, let me put it another way: Do you have kids? And more specifically, do you have teenagers? If so, you know what I'm talking about.

One of the downsides of the information age, in which we have our iPhones, BlackBerrys, Treos, and other devices that can send and receive the latest data, is that we are constantly barraged by information. This information gives us even more to stress out about. And stress is serious stuff. Studies have suggested that high levels of stress can lead to obesity and trigger a raft of diseases, from heart attacks to ulcers. Depression, nervous breakdowns, and even cancer can be stress related. In the United States, up to 90 percent of visits to physicians may be triggered by a stress-related illness, according to the Centers for Disease Control and Prevention.[1]

We all stress out about the many frightening things in our world today. Since 9/11, there are certain fears all Americans share. A March 2005 Associated Press article stated, "Though the Soviet Union is gone, the nuclear fears that fueled the Cold War haven't disappeared. Most Americans think nuclear weapons are so dangerous that no country should have them."[2]

North Korea claims to possess nuclear weapons and to be manufacturing more. Iran is widely believed to be within months of developing such weapons. And lurking in the background is the threat that worries U.S. officials the most: the desire on the part of terrorists to acquire nuclear weapons. Fifty-three percent of Americans think a nuclear attack by terrorists is at least somewhat likely.[3]

That brings us stress, worry, and fear.

You may know someone who has a fear of heights, small spaces, or flying. But according to a *Time* magazine cover article on the topic of fear, people have phobias for just about everything imaginable. According to the article, over fifty million people in the U.S. have some kind of fear or phobia. Some are pretty unusual, if not slightly humorous. For example, there is kathisophobia, the fear of sitting; ablutophobia, the fear of bathing; dentophobia, the fear of dentists; allodoxaphobia, the fear of opinions; and cyclophobia, the fear of bicycles.

And they get even weirder. There is alektorophobia, the fear of chickens; anuptaphobia, the fear of staying single; arachibutyrophobia, the fear of peanut butter sticking to the roof of your mouth; automatonophobia, the fear of ventriloquist dummies; ecclesiophobia, the fear of church; ouranophobia, the fear of heaven; and peladophobia, the fear of baldness and/or bald people.

Finally, there is my personal favorite: phobophobia, which is the fear of phobias.[4]

Perhaps your life is filled with fear, worry, and intense stress of some kind right now. Without a doubt, life is certainly filled with troubles. The book of Job tells us, "Man is born to trouble" (Job 5:7).

Disappointment is a trouble, and in life there are many disappointments. We are disappointed with ourselves, because we are not always what we want to be. We want to be strong, but we are weak. We want to be successful, yet we experience many failures. We want to be loved, but people are often indifferent toward us.

Circumstances can also be a source of trouble: the loss of a job, relationship issues, events not going the way we want them to, or even uncertainty about the future. All these things can cause us stress and fear.

But my intention here is not to add to your stress. Instead, I want to share with you the words of Jesus to a stressed-out, agitated people.

This is God's cure for heart trouble:

> "Let not your heart be troubled; you believe in God, believe also in Me. In My Father's house are many mansions; if it were not so, I would have told you. I go to prepare a place for you. And if I go and prepare a place for you, I will come again and receive you to Myself; that where I am, there you may be also. And where I go you know, and the way you know." Thomas said to Him, "Lord, we do not know where You are going, and how can we

know the way?" Jesus said to him, "I am the way, the truth, and the life. No one comes to the Father except through Me." (John 14:1–6)

When Jesus spoke these words, His disciples were afraid.

He had just revealed that Judas Iscariot would betray Him, and that Simon Peter would deny Him. Then He dropped the bombshell: He was going to leave them! They didn't understand that He would die on the cross for them and that He would soon live in their hearts. They only heard the part about Him leaving.

And that caused stress, worry, and fear. So the phrase He utters, *let not your heart be troubled*, in verse 1 could be translated, "Don't be agitated, disturbed, or thrown into confusion." Or, "Don't let your heart shudder!" Or even more casually, "Relax!" *Troubled* is a strong word. Jesus told the disciples, in light of the imminent cross, "It may look like your world is falling apart and that darkness will overtake you, but don't let your heart be troubled!" Notice that Jesus didn't say, "Mull over your problems a bit." Instead, He said, "Don't be troubled." And then He laid out three reasons why.

As Christians, regardless of what cause we may have to be troubled, there is *greater cause not to be.*

This brings us to God's first cure for heart trouble: *His Word is true.* Jesus said, "Believe also in Me" (John 14:1). In the original Greek, this is a command. Jesus tells them, "Believe that I know what I'm doing here! My Word is true. You will see that in time."

God has given us a user's manual for life called the Bible. Now, I don't know about you, but I hate to read user's manuals. This is a problem, because I also love electronic gadgets. If you're like me, you try out your gadgets first and read the directions later (and usually end up doing the first thing the user's manual told you *not* to do!).

While many products come with user's manuals, some products also come with warning labels. Some warning labels are helpful, others seem just plain ridiculous. But we all know those ridiculous labels are there because *someone,* somewhere, did what the label warns you *not* to do.

Consider these goofy but real warning labels. A cardboard sunshade for windshields had this warning: "Do not drive with sun shield in place." This warning came with a hair dryer: "Do not use while sleeping." An electric rotary tool included the caution, "This product not intended for use as a dental drill." A warning on a bathroom heater stated, "This product is not to be used in bathrooms." A manual for a microwave oven contained this warning: "Do not use for drying pets." This statement was found on a box of rat poison: "Warning: has been found to cause cancer in laboratory mice." A warning label on children's cough medicine cautions, "Do not drive or operate machinery." A string of Christmas lights was intended "For indoor or outdoor use only." A child-sized Superman costume came with this warning: "Wearing of this garment does not enable you to fly." A sign at a railroad station declared, "Beware! To touch these wires is instant death. Anyone found doing so will be prosecuted." A shipment of hammers came with the notice, "May be harmful if swallowed." And a bottle of sleeping pills forewarned, "May cause drowsiness."

Think of the people who tried to blow dry their hair while they were asleep, swallow a hammer, or fly because they wore *S* on their chests. If only they had read the directions and warning labels first!

The same is true of life. The Bible gives us directions and warnings to guide us. In 2 Timothy 3:16–17 we read, "All Scripture is inspired by God and is useful to teach us what is true and to make us realize what is wrong in our lives. It corrects us when we are wrong and teaches us to do what is right. God uses it to prepare and equip his people to do every good work" (NLT).

This passage reminds me of a story I heard about a young man who was graduating from college. His father hoped to give his son a new car for his graduation present. Many of the other graduates were getting new cars from their dads, so this young man wanted one too. He had even picked out the car he wanted and told his father about it.

When the day of his graduation finally arrived, his dad shocked the young man when he did not hand him car keys, but rather, a brand-new Bible. The son was so outraged that he turned and walked away, leaving his father holding the Bible. In fact, he was so bitter, he cut off all contact with his father and never spoke to him again.

When the father died, the young man went to his house to prepare for the funeral and to help get his father's affairs in order. There, sitting on a shelf, he noticed the Bible his father had given him for his graduation years before. He blew off the dust and, with tears in his eyes, opened it for the first time. Much to his astonishment, he found an envelope tucked inside the Bible with his name on it. Inside was a cashier's check, made out to him, for the exact price of the car he had picked out. The check was dated the day of his graduation.

His father gave him the car he wanted, but he had to open the
Bible to get it. He never realized what his father had done for him,
because he did not open his Bible.

As sad as that story is, we essentially do the same thing when
we never open the Book our heavenly Father gave to us. Inside this
book is something far more valuable than a cashier's check. The Bible
contains the words of life. In it we find the truth about how to get
to heaven.

What could be more valuable than that?

God's second cure for heart trouble is this: *We are going to heaven.*
Jesus said, "In My Father's house are many mansions" (John 14:2).
This is only true for the people who put their faith in Christ. The
unbeliever does not have the promise of heaven. No matter what
happens to you on this earth, it pales in comparison to this great
hope.

As 2 Corinthians 4:17–18 tells us,

> For our present troubles are small and won't last
> very long. Yet they produce for us a glory that vastly
> outweighs them and will last forever! So we don't
> look at the troubles we can see now; rather, we fix
> our gaze on things that cannot be seen. For the
> things we see now will soon be gone, but the things
> we cannot see will last forever. (NLT)

Deep inside, we all *long* for this place we have never been. C. S.
Lewis called this "the inconsolable longing." He said, "There have
been times when I think we do not desire heaven; but more often I

find myself wondering whether, in our heart of hearts, we have ever desired anything else."[5] We all have a longing for heaven, whether we know it or not.

Heaven is waiting for the children of God; you have His word on it. And there is only one thing that God cannot do, and that is lie. Jesus has gone to prepare a place for us (John 14:2). And this is a key element of our comfort. When you have guests stay in your home, you prepare the room for them. You might know they like certain books or treats, so maybe you customize the room. You do this so that when your guests arrive, they will feel at home.

In the same way, God prepares a place for you.

I heard about an eighty-five-year-old couple who had been married for almost sixty years before they were killed in a car accident. They were in good health over the last ten years of their lives, mainly as a result of her interest in healthy food and exercise. When they reached the pearly gates, St. Peter took them to their mansion, which was decked out with a beautiful kitchen and a master suite, complete with a sauna and Jacuzzi. As they ooh'ed and aah'ed over their new residence, the man asked Peter how much all this would cost.

"It's free," Peter replied. "This is heaven."

Next, they went outside to survey the championship golf course behind their new home. They would have golfing privileges every day, and each week, the course would change, allowing members to play one of the great golf courses on earth.

The man asked, "What are the green fees?"

"This is heaven," said Peter. "You play for free!"

Then, they went to the clubhouse and saw the lavish buffet lunch with the finest cuisines of the world laid out.

"How much to eat?" asked the man.

"Don't you understand yet? This is heaven," Peter replied, with some exasperation. "It's free!"

"Well, where are the low-fat and low-cholesterol tables?" the man asked.

"That's the best part," Peter replied. "You can eat as much as you like of whatever you like, and you never get fat, and you never get sick. This is heaven!"

With that, the man threw down his hat, stomped on it, and screamed wildly. Both his wife and Peter tried to calm him down, asking what was wrong.

The man looked at his wife and said, "This is all *your* fault! If it weren't for your blasted bran muffins, I could have been here ten years ago!"

I don't believe that the description of mansions in heaven is literal in the sense of a Beverly Hills–type mansion. Rather, I think the mansions we hear spoken about in the Bible refer to the new bodies God will give to us when we get to heaven.

The Bible says in 2 Corinthians 5:1–2, "For we know that when this earthly tent we live in is taken down (that is, when we die and leave this earthly body), we will have a house in heaven, an eternal body made for us by God himself and not by human hands. We grow weary in our present bodies, and we long to put on our heavenly bodies like new clothing" (NLT).

Our hearts should not be troubled because *His Word is true* and *we are going to heaven*. God's final cure for heart trouble is this: *He is coming back for us*. We read in John 14:3, "And if I go and prepare a place for you, I will come again and receive you to Myself; that where I am, there you may be also." In our fallen world, we find relief for our troubled hearts in the promise that Jesus will come back to receive us unto Himself.

When General Douglas MacArthur left the Philippines in the early months of World War II, he fled Corregidor in apparent defeat. Upon reaching Australia, he sent back the now-famous declaration, "I shall return!" And he kept his promise. Three years later, he stood on Philippine soil and made his second historic statement, "I have returned!"[6]

Jesus told us that He will come again, and someday, in the not-too-distant future, He will set foot on planet earth once again and say, "I have returned."

And it may be sooner than we think. The Lord Jesus will not merely send for us, but will come in person to escort us to His Father's house. In 1 Thessalonians 4:16–18 we read,

> For the Lord Himself will descend from heaven with a shout, with the voice of an archangel, and with the trumpet of God. And the dead in Christ will rise first. Then we who are alive and remain shall be caught up together with them in the clouds to meet the Lord in the air. And thus we shall always be with the Lord. Therefore comfort one another with these words.

Notice that Jesus does not say that He will take us to Himself, rather He will "receive us" (John 14:3). It is not something that He will do against our will. He will return for those who are watching and waiting. Not just the place, heaven, but the person, Jesus, will be ours!

These three reasons, or three cures for heart trouble, that Jesus offered can comfort and strengthen you:

1. His Word is true.
2. We are going to heaven.
3. He is coming back for us.

These promises were made only to the children of God who have received Christ.

Jesus revealed these truths to His disciples with this somewhat mysterious statement: "'And where I go you know, and the way you know'" (John 14:4). I think Jesus wanted them to ask what He meant. But Thomas was the only one bold enough to do so.

Thomas has been given the title "Doubting Thomas," but he was really more of a skeptic. The doubter doubts, even when the facts are clear, while the skeptic looks carefully, wanting to see the truth for himself or herself. Thomas wasn't one to let others do his thinking for him. He behaved more like "Honest Thomas" when he said, "Lord, we do not know where You are going, and how can we know the way?" (John 14:5).

It seems to me that the disciples acted as though they understood when they did not. Thomas was honest enough to speak out and say, "But I don't know where You are going!"

Aren't you glad Thomas said that? Thomas didn't understand and said so, causing Jesus to utter this incredible statement, one of His most famous and profound statements in all of Scripture. Jesus did not rebuke Thomas, but rather took his question as an opportunity to expand His revelation.

Jesus said to Thomas, "I am the way, the truth, and the life. No one comes to the Father except through Me" (John 14:6).

This statement is one of the most, if not *the* most, controversial aspects of our faith. By believing this, we are saying that *Jesus Christ is the only way to God.* The majority of Americans today do not hold this belief.

But if you believe the words of Jesus and think and act biblically, then you must believe that Jesus Christ's finished work on the cross is the reason you will get to heaven.

As Titus 3:5 says, "Not by works of righteousness which we have done, but according to His mercy He saved us, through the washing of regeneration and renewing of the Holy Spirit." And Acts 4:12 tells us, "Nor is there salvation in any other, for there is no other name under heaven given among men by which we must be saved." Then in 1 Timothy 2:5 we read, "For there is one God and one Mediator between God and men, the Man Christ Jesus."

"But that is being so narrow-minded!" some would say. "As long as people are sincere in their beliefs, they can follow any path they want."

What would you think of an airline pilot who announced just before takeoff, "Ladies and Gentlemen, welcome to flight 293 bound for Honolulu. Our cruising altitude today will be thirty-two thousand feet, and we will be showing an in-flight movie. By the way, I am not sure about this whole fuel thing. I see the gauge is indicating that we don't have enough fuel to reach our destination. But I feel good about this, so don't panic.

"Also, I am not really using our navigation devices or any maps today, because I feel that is too narrow a mind-set. We'll just flow with it, because after all, all roads lead to Hawaii.

"One last thing, folks. Don't worry, because I'm very sincere!"

All I would want to know at that point is, "How can I get off this plane? There is a psycho in the cockpit." Of course, we know it is serious business to pilot a plane. Yet how much more serious is our eternal destiny?

God has the cure for your heart trouble. He has the answer to all your questions. He is the way for you to get to heaven. So, what do you need to do to know with certainty that you're going there?

First, realize that you are a sinner. Every one of us has broken God's commandments. The Bible says, "For all have sinned and fall short of the glory of God" (Rom. 3:23). The Greek word translated as *sin* means "to fall short of a standard" or "to miss the mark." We have all fallen short of God's standards, because the Bible says, "Be perfect, just as your Father in heaven is perfect" (Matt. 5:48). Who is perfect? *Not one of us.*

It also means no more excuses. Stop blaming your parents, addictive behavior, or someone or something else. Like one man in the Bible, you need to say, "God, be merciful to me!" (Luke 18:13).

Second, recognize that Jesus died on the cross for you. When the movie *The Passion of the Christ* was released, there was considerable controversy over who was responsible for the death of Jesus. *Newsweek* magazine ran a cover article entitled "Who Killed Jesus?" The debate raged. Who was really responsible? Do we put the blame on the Romans? Do we put the blame on the Jewish people? I thought the debate was absurd, because I will tell you who killed Jesus: *I did. You did.* Our sins did. And more to the point, Jesus did not go to the cross against His will. He willingly went, because there was no other way to satisfy the demands of a righteous God, whom we offended. Nails did not hold Jesus to the cross of Calvary. Love did—love for you and love for me.

Jesus said, "Greater love has no one than this, than to lay down one's life for his friends" (John 15:13). No one forced Him to go to that cross. Christ willingly died for our sins.

Third, repent of your sin. The Bible says that God "commands all people everywhere to repent" (Acts 17:30 NIV). This is missing in many people's so-called conversions. It is not enough to be sorry for doing something wrong. We must also be sorry enough to change our ways.

So if you want to get right with God, let go of your sins. You need to be willing to follow Him and do what He has called you to do.

Fourth, receive Christ into your life. Salvation comes not just by believing that He is the Son of God, but by receiving Him into your life. Jesus said, "Behold, I stand at the door and knock. If anyone hears My voice and opens the door, I will come in to him and dine with him, and he with Me" (Rev. 3:20). And John 1:12 says, "But as many as received Him, to them He gave the right to become children of God, to those who believe in His name." You see, there has to come a moment when you say, "Lord, forgive me of my sin. Come into my life." *I can't do that for you.* Another Christian can't do that for you. You have to say, "Lord, I need Your forgiveness." You must receive Him.

Fifth, do it publicly. Jesus said, "Whoever confesses Me before men, him I will also confess before My Father who is in heaven"

(Matt. 10:32). But He also said, "Whoever denies Me before men, him I will also deny before My Father who is in heaven" (Matt. 10:33). The point is this: If you want to be a true follower of Jesus, you need to do it in a public way.

Sixth, do it now. The Bible says, "Behold, now is the accepted time; behold, now is the day of salvation" (2 Cor. 6:2), reflecting the earlier command, "Seek the LORD while He may be found, call upon Him while He is near" (Isa. 55:6).

The Lord is here with us right now. He is calling us to Himself. There are some of you who need to get right with God, and I am going to give you an opportunity to do that as we continue. There are some of you who have fallen away from the Lord and need to come back to Him. Later, I will give you an opportunity to return to Christ, if you haven't already.

2

EVERYDAY JESUS

Can you think of a person you could never imagine as a Christian, someone so hardened, so resistant, and so far gone that he or she would never follow Jesus Christ? Or perhaps *you* are such a person. Or at least you think you are. Maybe you feel as though you wouldn't qualify to follow Jesus.

I was such a person.

I was raised in a home plagued by divorce and alcoholism. "The OC" was my stomping ground. I went to school at Newport Harbor High in Newport Beach, California. I got into the party scene, drugs, and drinking, and then suddenly, I came to know Jesus. I can tell you, it was the last thing I ever planned on doing, but thankfully, God had different plans. My conversion was so unexpected that people didn't believe that Greg Laurie had become a Christian. Yet when I look back on the decision I made and how some of my friends from those earlier days did *not* make the same decision, I have no regrets whatsoever—not a single one.

Make no mistake about it: Conversion is instantaneous.

While the process of growing and maturing spiritually takes a lifetime, the actual work of conversion can take just seconds. If you don't believe me, just think of Christians you know. How many have had their lives changed?

Briefly, I want to tell you the story of a man whose life was dramatically changed after one short encounter with Jesus. He was a man who left his career, wealth, and power simply to become a follower of Jesus. It all happened when he came face-to-face with Jesus Christ, who said two words: "Follow Me."

His name was Matthew, and this is his story:

> As Jesus was walking along, he saw a man named Matthew sitting at his tax collector's booth. "Follow me and be my disciple," Jesus said to him. So Matthew got up and followed him.
>
> Later, Matthew invited Jesus and his disciples to his home as dinner guests, along with many tax collectors and other disreputable sinners. But when the Pharisees saw this, they asked his disciples, "Why does your teacher eat with such scum?"
>
> When Jesus heard this, he said, "Healthy people don't need a doctor—sick people do." (Matt. 9:9–12 NLT)

I don't know about you, but there are two places I don't like to go: the doctor's office and the dentist's office. And I only go as a last resort, especially to the dentist. It is probably because I'm afraid of hearing bad news.

Somehow, we mistakenly believe that ignorance is bliss.

A man named Phil went to the doctor, and after a long check-up, his doctor said, "I have some bad news for you. You don't have long to live."

"How long do I have?" asked Phil.

"Ten," the doctor said.

"Ten *what?* Months? Days?"

The doctor interrupted him, "Nine, eight, seven …"

But back to our story.

In Jesus' time, people hated tax collectors. For one thing, they collected taxes from their own fellow Jews *for the Romans,* who were the occupying power in Israel at the time. To make matters worse, tax collectors would often skim off the top or charge more than was required and pocket the profits. The primary reason the Jews hated Matthew is because they saw him as a turncoat and a collaborator with Rome. It would be akin to an American collecting intelligence for Al-Qaeda. Matthew had aligned himself with the enemies of his own people. It's as though he had gone out of his way to offend his fellow Jews—*and God.*

We all know people who will go far out of their way to offend and upset others. Sometimes this can be a cry for attention. And sometimes they are running from what they know is right.

But why had Matthew, also known as Levi, chosen this lifestyle that would alienate and offend so many? We don't know, but we do know this: He was most likely hated by all—all except Jesus, that is. Matthew's only "friends" would have been other tax collectors.

Maybe you feel as though you are hated. Maybe you are lonely, and you don't even know if you have any real friends. Do you hate the course your life has taken? Perhaps you are into drugs, drinking, partying, or something else. You feel as though life has "chewed you up and spit you out." Or maybe you have thought, *If only I could make the big bucks, then I would be happy.*

As hip-hop star Eminem once said in an interview, "You gotta be careful what you wish for. I always wished and hoped for this. But it's almost turning into more of a nightmare than a dream." He explained that he can't walk down the street anymore, and said, "To be honest, I really didn't have much support ... just a few friends. And just myself."[1]

And rapper Bow Wow, estimated to be worth more than $50 million, said, "I found out the hard way that you can have everything in the world and still not be satisfied."[2]

Musician Dave Matthews makes $20 million a year from his music and touring, but is he a happy guy? In an interview with *Rolling Stone,* Matthews admitted to being suicidal: "It comes and goes. I don't think that it will ever end. When things inside your head get kind of crazy, and you go, 'OK, let's go through the list of options ...'" He continued, "I like to drink, a lot—I think it's a healthy thing to do. But I've got a family; and I've got other things that impress me more than another drink.... I may pause, but I don't think I'll ever stop, because forever is a long time."[3]

The lyrics to one of his songs, "Trouble," perhaps explain why he feels this way:

> My empty heart begs you
> Leave me be ...
> You know too well

> That I have fallen
> Pray your mercy give to me.[4]

Matthew the tax collector was once a wealthy and successful man, but he wasn't happy either. And he had turned his back on the very One who could help him: God. Matthew had been raised to believe, but he turned away.

It's amazing how many people will turn away from God at an early age because a minister, priest, or person claiming to be a Christian did not behave as one. People will turn away from the gospel of Jesus today for the same reasons. In fact, there are two reasons people don't go to church:

1. They don't know a Christian.
2. They *do* know a Christian.

I apologize for all the Christians who have not been good representatives of Jesus Christ. But we have to keep in mind that Jesus did not say to Matthew, "Follow My people."

Rather, He said, "Follow Me." And He says that to you as well. I have been a follower of Jesus for well over thirty years now, and I can tell you He has never been inconsistent in any way. Sure, fellow Christians have disappointed me at times (and I'm sure I've disappointed others as well), but Jesus Christ has always been who He promised to be.

Matthew would have had a great seat at his strategically located tax booth. He may even have listened as Jesus taught from a boat. His hardened and bitter heart began to soften. But he couldn't bring himself to get up from that tax booth and go to Jesus. He probably was afraid Jesus would reject him: "Do I actually look so desperate that I would want a tax collector to follow Me?"

I used to be like Matthew.

I would hang out in Newport Beach, just wishing some Christian would talk to me, but none of them ever did. Thankfully, God saw past my hardened facade and called my name—just as He called Matthew's, and just as He now calls yours.

You may be thinking, *But I'm just not the religious type.* Well, good news, God isn't looking for the religious type. He's looking for the sinner type.

One day, Jesus saw Matthew and forever changed the tax collector's life: "As Jesus passed on from there, He saw a man named Matthew sitting at the tax office. And He said to him, 'Follow Me.' So he arose and followed Him" (Matt. 9:9). The word *saw* in this verse is very suggestive. It means "to gaze intently upon, to stare, to fix one's eyes constantly upon an object." I'm sure that when people walked by Matthew, normally they would either turn away their eyes or look at him with scorn.

This word also means "to look right through."

Have you ever had someone look right through you? Or, let me put it another way: Jesus intentionally made eye contact with Matthew. And in the eyes of Jesus, Matthew saw many things: holiness and purity, to name two. But I'm certain he also saw love, compassion, and understanding. With their eyes fixed on each other, Jesus said two words that would reverberate through Matthew's soul, words that he never thought he would hear: "Follow Me." Jesus chose, selected, and called him out to be His disciple. And Jesus says the same thing to you right now.

But what does it mean to "follow Jesus"?

There are a lot of us today who claim to be His followers, but do we really follow Him? As 2 Corinthians 13:5 reminds us, "Examine and test and evaluate your own selves to see whether you are holding to your faith and showing the proper fruits of it. Test and prove yourselves [not Christ]. Do you not yourselves realize and know [thoroughly by an ever-increasing experience] that Jesus Christ is in you—unless you are [counterfeits] disapproved on trial and rejected?" (AB).

This phrase *follow Me* could also be translated, "follow *with* Me," meaning companionship and friendship. Jesus was saying, "Matthew, I want you to be My friend!" Jesus wants you to bare your heart to Him, to tell Him your secrets, your fears, your hopes, and your dreams. Jesus said, "You are My friends if you do whatever I command you. No longer do I call you servants, for a servant does not know what his master is doing; but I have called you friends, for all things that I heard from My Father I have made known to you" (John 15:14–15).

Many people think God is out to ruin their lives. Some believe God is always mad at them. Such was the case with a burglar who broke into a house one night. As he quietly made his way around, a voice suddenly spoke through the darkness:

"I see you, and Jesus sees you too."

He stopped, amazed at what he had just heard. He waited for a few moments, and when nothing happened, he continued on.

A second time the voice said, "I see you, and Jesus sees you too."

Stunned, the burglar turned on his flashlight for a look around the room. To his surprise and relief, he saw a large birdcage in the corner with a parrot inside.

"Did you say that?" he asked the parrot.

"I see you, and Jesus sees you too," the parrot repeated for the third time.

"Why, it's a parrot!" laughed the burglar. But then the burglar saw a large Doberman with its teeth bared, looking at him.

The parrot then said to the Doberman, "Sic 'em, Jesus!"

That's how a lot of people see Jesus: ready to pounce on them and ruin their lives. Nothing could be further from the truth. The fact is, God loves you, and His plan for you is good. God says, "For I know the thoughts that I think toward you, says the LORD, thoughts of peace and not of evil, to give you a future and a hope" (Jer. 29:11).

As in the story of the prodigal son, when we sin against God, He misses us, just as the father missed his wayward son. God wants to be your friend. The question is, do you want to be His?

There are a lot of people running around today who claim to be friends of Jesus. But if you are a true friend of Jesus, then you will obey Him. Remember, Jesus said, "You are My friends if you do whatever I *command* you" (John 15:14). It's not for us to choose which parts of the Bible we like and throw out the rest.

God offers us a package deal.

When Jesus said to Matthew, "Follow Me," the word *follow* comes from a Greek word meaning "to walk the same road." Jesus' statement was not only an invitation, but a command that implied continuity. Jesus was essentially saying, "I command you to follow Me each and every day."

Following Jesus is not something we do only on Sunday. He wants to go with you to church, to school, to work, to the movies, as you surf the Internet, and wherever you go.

The Bible tells us that Matthew "arose and followed Him" (Matt. 9:9). Luke's gospel adds this detail: "So he [Matthew] left all, rose up, and followed Him" (Luke 5:28).

Matthew, recognizing the privilege being offered to him, stood up without hesitation and followed Jesus. Do you realize what a privilege it is that Jesus is calling you today?

You may wonder, *If I follow Jesus, will I have to give up anything?*

You will give up emptiness, loneliness, guilt, and the fear of death. In their places, Jesus will give you fulfillment, friendship, forgiveness, and the guarantee of heaven when you die. It is God's "trade-in deal," and it is here for you right now.

It would be like hearing a knock at your front door.

"Who is it?" you call out.

"It's Jesus!" a voice replies. "I stand at the door and knock, and if you will hear My voice and open the door, I will come in!"

You quickly open the door, and there He stands: Jesus Christ. You invite Him into your front room.

Nervously you ask, "Could I get you something to eat, Jesus?"

"Of course. Thank you," He answers.

You rush into your kitchen, open the door to the refrigerator, and see only day-old pizza and a few deviled eggs. Somehow those do not seem appropriate. As you think about what to give Jesus to eat, you hear noise coming from the front room, so you run back in. There stands Jesus, taking down your pictures from the wall. In the short time you were out of the room, He has already thrown all your furniture onto the front lawn.

Then He tears up your carpet—so you cry out, "Jesus, with all due respect, what are You doing?"

"A little spring-cleaning," He responds.

"But Jesus, this is all my stuff here, and frankly, if I would have known You were going to get rid of it, I might not have let You in!"

He ignores your outburst and whistles to the large moving truck backing up to your driveway.

"Bring it in, boys!" Jesus calls.

Two very large men lay down the most beautiful carpet you have ever seen. Then they begin to put up color-coordinated, lush wall coverings. Then new works of art are hung in the place of your old ones.

"You have good taste, Jesus!"

"Yes. Don't forget, I created the heavens and earth," He answers.

"Good point, Lord!" you respond.

Gorgeous, handcrafted furniture is carefully laid on your new carpet, and suddenly it dawns on you: Jesus only took away the old things to put something better in their place.

When a person meets Jesus Christ, he or she cannot leave the old life fast enough. Old habits, standards, and practices are gladly left behind. Far from being depressed about what he left behind, Matthew's heart overflowed with joy. He lost a career, but gained a destiny. He lost his material possessions, but gained a spiritual fortune. He lost his temporary security, but gained eternal life. He gave up all this world had to offer, but found Jesus.

You may be like Matthew. Maybe you don't have many friends. Maybe you feel alone and empty.

Jesus is looking at you right now and saying, "Follow Me."

He offers you forgiveness for sins, the hope of heaven, and peace instead of turmoil. He offers you friendship and companionship instead of loneliness. He offers you heaven instead of hell. But you must come to Him—not tomorrow, not next week, month, or year, but this moment. Jesus is saying to you right now, "Follow Me."

You may think, *God could never change someone like me!* But He can—and He will. The Bible says, "Therefore, if anyone is in Christ, he is a new creation; the old has gone, the new has come!" (2 Cor. 5:17 NIV). Would you like a fresh start? A new beginning? Would you like never to be alone again?

Or have you, like Matthew, fallen away from the faith? Are you living in such a way that if Christ were to return, you wouldn't be ready? God says, "Return, you backsliding children, and I will heal your backslidings" (Jer. 3:22).

You can come back to Christ today.

3

FAMOUS LAST WORDS

For every person there will come a last meal, a last breath, and of course, last words. And in many ways, what we say in the end is a real insight into who we were in life, what we stood for, and what we lived for. Generally, we die as we lived.

I read about a man who had been very successful in the restaurant business. On his deathbed with his family gathered nearby, he gave his last whisper: "Slice the ham thin!" And the last words of the famous writer Oscar Wilde were, "Either that wallpaper goes, or I do."

Sometimes, people know they are speaking their last words. Before he was to be hanged for spying on the British, the last words of American patriot Nathan Hale were: "I only regret that I have but one life to lose for my country."

And at other times, people don't know when they will be giving their last words. William "Buckey" O'Neil was an Arizona lawyer, newspaperman, sheriff, congressman, and one of the most important members of Teddy Roosevelt's Rough Riders during the Spanish-American War. Just prior to the famous charge up Kettle

Hill, O'Neil was standing up, smoking a cigarette, and joking with his troops while under fire from the ridge. One of his sergeants shouted to him above the noise, "Captain, a bullet is sure to hit you!"

O'Neil shouted back: "Sergeant, the Spanish bullet isn't made that will kill me!" No sooner had O'Neil uttered those words than he was hit and killed by a bullet.

Death is no respecter of persons, even of royalty. On her death-bed, Elizabeth I, Queen of England, said, "All my possessions for a moment of time." And Princess Diana, following that horrific car accident in a Paris tunnel, was heard to say, "My God! What happened?"

History tells the story of the renowned atheist Voltaire who wrote many things to undermine the church and said of Jesus Christ, "Curse the wretch.... In twenty years, Christianity will be no more. My single hand will destroy the edifice it took twelve apostles to rear."[1] Needless to say, Voltaire was less than successful. The physician with Voltaire at his death said that he cried out with utter despera-tion, "I am abandoned by God and man. I will give you half of what I am worth if you will give me six month's life." When the physician replied that he would not live six weeks, Voltaire proclaimed, "Then I shall go to hell and you will go with me." He exclaimed, "O Christ! O Jesus Christ!"[2]

What a difference faith makes. The last words of Stephen, who was being stoned to death, were "Lord Jesus, receive my spirit.... Lord, do not charge them with this sin" (Acts 7:59–60).

Now let's consider the most famous and important "last words" ever uttered: the words of Jesus as He hung on the cross. I want to focus on one statement in particular, for in it we see God's most painful moment.

Death by crucifixion was really death by suffocation. It was extremely hard even to breathe, much less speak. Add to this the fact that Jesus had been brutally whipped. This process was barbaric. The prisoner was tied to a post with his hands over his head, his body stretched taut. The whip had a short wooden handle with several leather thongs attached, each tipped with sharp pieces of metal or bone. As the whip was brought down on the prisoner, his muscles would be lacerated, veins and arteries would be torn open, and even the kidneys, spleen, or other organs could be exposed and slashed.

As Jesus hung on that cross, next to Him hung two criminals being crucified for their crimes. Jesus, on the other hand, was there for the crimes of all humanity. They were there against their wills. Yet Jesus willingly went. They could not have escaped. But He could have—with just one word to heaven. They were held to their crosses by nails. Jesus was held to His cross by love.

It's fascinating to see how these three men reacted as they looked death squarely in the face. As Jesus was nailed to the cross, these two men momentarily forgot their personal pain and joined the chorus of the onlookers' voices:

> "He saved others; Himself He cannot save.
> If He is the King of Israel, let Him now come
> down from the cross, and we will believe Him.
> He trusted in God; let Him deliver Him now if
> He will have Him; for He said, 'I am the Son of

God.'" Even the robbers who were crucified with
Him reviled Him with the same thing. (Matt.
27:42–44)

How this mockery and unbelief must have pained the heart of
Jesus. Even there at the cross, they persisted, while He atoned for the
very people who spewed this venom.

In Matthew's account, we read that both thieves joined the
crowd in mockery, yet Luke's gospel tells us that one of them rebuked
the other. Is this a contradiction? No, it is a conversion! Something
significant happened to change the heart of one of these thieves,
bringing him to his spiritual senses. Initially, he joined the chorus of
mockery toward Jesus but then, he watched with amazement as Jesus
suffered the same crucifixion he and the other thief had, yet without
any complaint, protest, or cursing.

Then came those unbelievable, unexpected, and incomprehen-
sible words of Christ: "Father, forgive them" (Luke 23:34). These
words reverberated through the thief's hardened heart! His rebellion,
bitterness, and anger dissolved. His heart *softened.*

While the first words Jesus uttered from the cross were a prayer
for His enemies, His next words were an answer to prayer, an answer
addressed to a single individual. Jesus spoke to him as though he
were the only person in the world. Luke's gospel tells us the believing
thief said, "'Jesus, remember me when you come into your kingdom.'
Jesus answered him, 'I tell you the truth, today you will be with me
in paradise'" (Luke 23:42–43 NIV).

In the same way, once you believe in Jesus, you can know you are
going to heaven. John said, "These things I have written to you who

believe in the name of the Son of God, that you may know that you have eternal life" (1 John 5:13).

Can you imagine the joy that must have filled the thief's heart in that moment?

There is much controversy about who is responsible for the death of Jesus Christ. Was it the Jewish Sanhedrin and the Pharisees? Was it the high priest, Caiaphas? Were the Romans responsible? Or Pilate?

While the debate continues, we know it was our sins that put Him on the cross. Because there was no other way to satisfy the demands of a holy God, Jesus, who was God, died in our place. The Bible says, "While we were still sinners, Christ died for us" (Rom. 5:8). And Paul wrote, "I live by faith in the Son of God, who loved me and gave Himself for me" (Gal. 2:20).

Finally, the tragedy of the crucifixion reached its horrific climax. In fact, it has been described as "the crucifixion in the crucifixion":

> Now from the sixth hour until the ninth hour there was darkness over all the land. And about the ninth hour Jesus cried out with a loud voice, saying, "Eli, Eli, lama sabachthani?" that is, *"My God, My God, why have You forsaken Me?"*
>
> Some of those who stood there, when they heard that, said, "This Man is calling for Elijah!" Immediately one of them ran and took a sponge, filled it with sour wine and put it on a reed, and offered it to Him to drink.
>
> The rest said, "Let Him alone; let us see if Elijah will come to save Him."

And Jesus cried out again with a loud voice,
and yielded up His spirit. (Matt. 27:45–50)

Without explanation, the sky turned dark. From the sixth hour (noon) to three o'clock in the afternoon, an ominous darkness fell across the land. The Greek word for "land" in this passage could be translated "earth," indicating the entire world. The darkness was then pierced by the voice of Jesus: "My God, My God, why have You forsaken Me?" (Matt. 27:46).

No fiction writer would have his or her hero say words like these. They surprise us, disarm us, and cause us to wonder what Jesus meant. We are looking at something that, in many ways, is impossible for humans to fathom. Clearly, we tread on holy ground when we look into such a subject, yet the impact on our lives is so significant that it certainly bears investigating. If we can gain a better understanding of what Jesus actually went through, it only gives us a greater appreciation for all He has done for us.

When Jesus uttered those words, they were not the delusions of a man in pain. His faith was not failing Him. After all, He cried out, "My God, My God …"

No, as Christ hung there, He bore the sins of the world. He was dying as a substitute for others. He suffered the punishment for all the world's sins on our behalf.

The very essence of the punishment was the outpouring of God's wrath against sinners. So in some mysterious way, which we may never fully comprehend, during those awful hours on the cross the Father poured out the full measure of His wrath against sin. And the recipient of that wrath was God's own beloved Son! God was punishing Jesus as though He had personally committed every wicked deed of every wicked sinner. And in doing so, He forgave all sinners as though they had lived Christ's perfect life of righteousness. Scripture says this clearly: "For He made Him who knew no sin *to be* sin for us, that we might become the righteousness of God in Him" (2 Cor. 5:21).

We also read in Isaiah 53:4–5:

> Surely He has borne our griefs
> And carried our sorrows;
> Yet we esteemed Him stricken,
> Smitten by God, and afflicted.
> But He was wounded for our transgressions,
> He was bruised for our iniquities;
> The chastisement for our peace was upon Him,
> And by His stripes we are healed.

Scripture tells us that "it pleased the LORD to bruise Him" (Isa. 53:10), and we also read that "[Christ] himself bore our sins in his body on the tree, so that we might die to sins and live for righteousness; by his wounds you have been healed" (1 Peter 2:24 NIV).

Sin was everywhere around Him at that dreaded moment. We cannot fathom what He went through. Jesus realized all our worst fears about the horrors of hell as He received the penalty for our wrongdoing.

But to be forsaken of God was an even greater source of anguish to Jesus, because He was absolutely, 100 percent holy. The physical pains of crucifixion, horrible as they were, were nothing compared to the wrath of the Father being poured out upon Him. This is why, in Gethsemane, "His sweat became like great drops of blood falling down to the ground" (Luke 22:44). This is why He looked ahead to the cross with such horror, because never, not for one moment during His entire earthly life, did He step outside of intimate fellowship with God.

Why, then, did this have to happen?

It had to happen because of the wall between God and humanity. God, in all His holiness, could not look at sin, because He is "of purer eyes than to behold evil, and cannot look on wickedness" (Hab. 1:13).

As a result, human beings in all their sinfulness could not look at God. So God had to turn His face and pour His wrath and judgment out upon His own Son. Understand that for Jesus, this was the greatest sacrifice He could have made. His greatest pain occurred at this moment. To have felt forsaken of God was the necessary consequence of sin. For a person to be forsaken of God is the penalty that follows a broken relationship with God. Jesus was forsaken so that I don't have to be. Jesus was forsaken for a time so that I might enjoy His presence forever. Jesus was forsaken so that I might be forgiven. Jesus entered the darkness so that I might walk in the light.

After this three-hour ordeal, Jesus gave His fifth statement from the cross and the first words of a personal nature: "I thirst!" (John 19:28). First, He prayed for His enemies, then for the thief on the cross, then He remembered His mother (John 19:26–27), expressed His forsakenness as He bore the sins of humanity, and finally He spoke of His own needs. Imagine the Creator of the universe making this statement—the One who created water! He could have so easily performed a miracle. He brought water out of rocks in the wilderness. His first earthly miracle was to turn water into wine at a wedding. He simply could have spoken water into existence.

But it's important to note that Jesus never once performed a miracle for His own benefit or comfort. When tempted by Satan to do this, He flat refused. Scripture tells us that He was hungry, He grew tired, He wept, and He was tempted in all ways as we are, yet He was still found without sin (Heb. 4:15). Yes, Jesus was 100 percent God, but He was also a man. He was not a man becoming God (that's impossible), but God who became a man. He was called "a Man of sorrows" (Isa. 53:3), so no matter how great your need or difficulty, you know He understands. You can cast "all your care upon Him, for He cares for you" (1 Peter 5:7). Is your body racked with pain? So was His. Have you ever been misunderstood, misjudged, or misrepresented? So was He. Have you had your closest friends turn away from you? So did His.

Jesus then uttered His sixth statement from the cross: "It is finished!" (John 19:30). The storm had finally passed, the cup had been drained. The devil had done his worst, and the Lord had bruised him. The darkness had ended.

The phrase *It is finished* is translated many ways: "It is made an end of"; "It is paid"; "It is performed"; or "It is accomplished."

What was made an end of? Our sins and the guilt that accompanied them.

What was paid? The price of redemption.

What was performed? The righteous requirements of the law.

What was accomplished? The work the Father had given Him to do.

Jesus Christ then rose from the dead. He is alive and here right now, wanting to come into your life.

We see three things as we look at the cross:

First, we see that it is a description of the depth of human sin. It has been said that you can tell the depth of a well by how much rope is lowered. So don't blame the people of that day for putting Jesus on the cross. You and I are just as guilty. It wasn't the Roman soldiers who killed Him; it was your sins and my sins that made it necessary for Him to volunteer for this torturous and humiliating death.

Second, in the cross we see the overwhelming love of God. If you are ever tempted to doubt God's love for you, just take a long look at the cross that He hung on for you. Romans 5:8 tells us, "But God demonstrates his own love for us in this: While we were still sinners, Christ died for us" (NIV).

Third, in the cross is the only way of salvation. Jesus said, "I am the way and the truth and the life. No one comes to the Father except through me" (John 14:6 NIV). If there had been any other way to save you, He would have found it. If living a good, moral life would save you, then Jesus never would have died. But He *did* die. Because there was—*and is*—no other way.

The short film *Most* is the story of a man who operates a drawbridge. At a certain time each afternoon, the man raised the bridge for a ferry, and then lowered it quickly for a passenger train that crossed a few minutes later.

One day, the man's young son visited him at work and decided to go down below to get a better look at the ferry as it passed. He accidently fell into the giant gears of the drawbridge and couldn't free himself.

The father now had to make the most difficult decision of his life. If he ran to free his son, the train would plunge into the river before the bridge could be lowered. But if he lowered the bridge to save the hundreds of passengers and crew on the train, his son would be crushed to death.

When he heard the train's whistle, the man knew what he had to do. With tears flowing down his cheeks, he pushed the master switch forward. As he looked up and watched the train rumble by, he saw the passengers casually going about their business. No one looked at the control house. No one cared that he had sacrificed his son.[3]

This is what happened at the cross of Calvary.

God sacrificed His Son for you because He loves you, because there was no other way for you to be forgiven of your sin. The Bible says, "For God so loved the world that He gave His only begotten Son, that whoever believes in Him should not perish but have everlasting life" (John 3:16).

4

HOW TO CHANGE YOUR LIFE

Without question, God loves you deeply and wants to reveal the personal, custom-made plan that He has for you. He wants to flood your life with peace and joy, and ultimately He wants to spend all eternity with you in heaven.

But just as surely as there is a loving God who cares for you, there is a hateful devil who wants to destroy you. He "prowls around like a roaring lion looking for someone to devour" (1 Peter 5:8 NIV). Jesus said that Satan comes "to steal and kill and destroy" (John 10:10 NIV).

On the other hand, Jesus says, "I have come that they may have life, and have it to the full" (John 10:10 NIV).

In Scripture we read the story of a man who had been taken over by the power of the devil, a tortured, suicidal, miserable, lonely shell of a man in an absolutely hopeless situation—that is, until Jesus came along.

It shows us the "package deal" Satan has in store for every person who is in his grip. First and foremost, he wants to keep you from coming to Jesus. He may entice you with all the glitz and glamour this world has to offer. He may reach you through greed for the acquisition of things. But once he has you where he wants you, he'll chew you up and spit you out.

Judas Iscariot is the classic example. It's hard to believe, but those thirty pieces of silver looked pretty appealing. Yet once the devil had what he wanted, he cast Judas aside like yesterday's garbage.

The stuff this world offers us can look so cool and attractive. MTV, for example, has mastered the practice of making bad stuff look good. One of their most popular shows of the recent past was *The Osbournes*. The head of the family is the wacky Ozzy Osbourne of Black Sabbath fame. Ozzy is the parent a lot of kids wish they had, because if some kid were to brag, "My dad started his own business," the kid with Ozzy for a father could say, "Oh yeah? Well, my dad bit the head off a bat!"

Ozzy and his wife, Sharon, have two kids, Kelly and Jack. Ozzy was a heavy drug user and drinker, but he told his kids not to follow his example. Nevertheless, Jack got caught up in drugs and drinking and, at age seventeen, entered a rehab facility to get help. Jack explained, "I got caught up in my new lifestyle and got carried away with drugs and alcohol."[1]

Do you think MTV was quick to do a clever show about Jack in rehab? Of course not, because they don't want you to see the reality of what sin can do. The world's idea of fulfillment is a complete rip-off, and the end result is frightening.

The story from Scripture illustrates these points. And in this story, we see three forces at work: Satan, society, and the Savior. We will see what Satan did in two men's lives, what society offered, and then what the Savior did:

> When [Jesus] arrived at the other side in the region of the Gadarenes, two demon-possessed men coming from the tombs met him. They were so violent that no one could pass that way. "What do you want with us, Son of God?" they shouted. "Have you come here to torture us before the appointed time?"
>
> Some distance from them a large herd of pigs was feeding. The demons begged Jesus, "If you drive us out, send us into the herd of pigs."
>
> He said to them, "Go!" So they came out and went into the pigs, and the whole herd rushed down the steep bank into the lake and died in the water. (Matt. 8:28–32 NIV)

As our story begins, we find two pathetic, demented men. In Luke's account of this story, he zeroes in on one of these men in particular. He seemed to be the more extreme of the two: "When [Jesus] stepped out on the land, there met Him a certain man from the city who had demons for a long time. And he wore no clothes, nor did he live in a house but in the tombs" (Luke 8:27). In addition to this, he would beat and bruise himself, cutting himself with sharp rocks. He was so strong that when he was put in chains, he broke them.

So here's a creepy scenario: a frightening, evil man with superhuman strength, who hangs around the graveyard. No doubt people avoided this place, especially at night. He was a dangerous man, but underneath that dark exterior was a truly tortured soul. As I mentioned earlier, he is a picture of Satan's ultimate goal—the finished product.

What steps led to this state we can only imagine. But here we see the "package deal" of sin, Satan, and death, all intertwined together in one man. Sin is indeed a living death, and the unbeliever is spiritually "dead in trespasses and sins" (Eph. 2:1). The Bible says, "The widow who lives for pleasure is dead even while she lives" (1 Tim. 5:6 NIV). But this is a story with a happy ending, because Jesus came into this poor, tortured man's life and made him an altogether different kind of person.

When Jesus showed up at this place seeking out these men, Satan reacted with force: "They began screaming at him, 'Why are you interfering with us, Son of God? Have you come here to torture us before God's appointed time?'" (Matt. 8:29 NLT). The power of Satan was so entwined with these men that most did not see the hurting people deep inside, only the crazed, suicidal maniacs roaming the graveyard. Yet in this cry, Jesus knew that they wanted His help.

Perhaps your friends have given you this book. You may have told them, "I don't need Jesus." There is an old proverb that says, "When you throw a rock into a pack of dogs, the one that barks the loudest is the one that got hit." Maybe that describes you right now. Despite all your arguments, you are reading this book—because deep down inside, you are searching.

James tells us that "even the demons believe—and tremble!" (James 2:19). It may surprise you to know that the demons, and the devil himself, are neither atheists nor agnostics. They believe in the existence of God. They believe in the deity of Jesus Christ. They know that the Bible is the Word of God. They believe Jesus is coming back again. Needless to say, they are not followers of Jesus.

In Luke's account of this story, we read that Jesus asked the man, "What is your name?" (Luke 8:30).

He answered, "Legion," because many demons had entered him. This man was so wrapped up in demonic power that he couldn't even answer for himself. A Roman legion consisted of six thousand soldiers, which could mean that thousands of demons had possessed this man!

Somewhere along the line, these men opened themselves up to satanic invasion. They played around with sin, and here we see sin playing around with them. They lost everything. They lost their homes, their family, their friends, and even their willpower. They fell completely under Satan's power. We must remember this when we start playing games with sin. Satan will dangle what he must in front of you to get you to take the bait.

People open the door to the supernatural through their use of drugs and the sin of sorcery. In fact, the Greek word *pharmakia,* translated as "witchcraft" or "sorcery," is the word from which our English word *pharmacy* is derived. The biblical definition of sorcery actually refers to the illicit use of drugs. When people use drugs, whether it's marijuana, cocaine, or any other mind-controlling substance, it opens them up to the dangers of the spiritual realm.

Dabbling in black magic, witchcraft, Ouija boards, or astrology can also open that door. The Bible tells us that "those who practice such things will not inherit the kingdom of God" (Gal. 5:21).

I did drugs and alcohol for a couple of years. I tried the party scene and thought that would do it. It only made my problems worse. I was trying to fill a hole in my heart that was made for God—not drugs, alcohol, sex, money, power, or anything else this world has to offer.

As I pointed out earlier, we see three forces at work in the story of the demon-possessed men: Satan, society, and the Savior. We've already seen what Satan did with these men. So what did society do for them? *They chained them up.*

Violent crime sweeps across our country every day. Law enforcement is often understaffed and underpaid. Many of our courts and judges give out lenient sentences. Gangs are growing and spreading. And sadly, the family is continuing to fall apart at an unprecedented rate. What is a society to do? Like those in Jesus' day, we just lock people up. With all of its wonderful scientific achievements, society still can't cope with the problems caused by Satan and sin.

In this story, no one could help these demon-possessed men either. Their situation seemed absolutely hopeless. But what the chains could not do, Jesus did with a word. This brings us to the third force at work in this story: *the Savior.*

What did Jesus do for these men? He found them in their spooky little graveyard and offered them hope. And apparently, these demons preferred inhabiting something instead of nothing, so Jesus sent them into a herd of pigs. The pigs all went over the cliff in madness.

Luke's account of this story tells us what happened to the man who was delivered: "Then they went out to see what had happened, and came to Jesus, and found the man from whom the demons had departed, sitting at the feet of Jesus, clothed and in his right mind" (Luke 8:35).

What a change!

In the same way, you can see changes in some Christians—they are so different from who they were before, you would never know their past. If you want proof of the existence of God, just look at the changes He has made in the lives of Christians you know.

I recently met a man from the Czech Republic who shared with me how Christ had changed his life. He told me,

> I grew up in the Czech Republic and in a family where my father was an alcoholic. My first drunkenness occurred when I was three years old, when my father left me in a room with glasses of liquor while he was partying with another guy. They took me to a hospital and found that I had been drunk for fifty hours and had almost died. I grew up in the communist system. It gave me a rough, hard, and angry attitude. Soon I was known as a fist fighter and an angry man. As I got older, I became even more violent. I went into the military. I spent a short time in prison for violence, alcoholism, and drunkenness.

He then explained that he moved to the United States and moved in with a girl. He went on to say:

> I continued my spiral into alcohol and all the rest of it. On one occasion, my life was spinning down into the bottomless pit. I lost fifty pounds and was ready to commit suicide. I was staring at a gun I was pointing in my mouth. I didn't have any resolve

to live. My whole life was one big emptiness, only existing, just a waste of time.

Here is this man, hopeless, alcoholic, violent, and suicidal. And what happened? He continued,

> At that time, my neighbor in Mission Viejo and her friends invited me to the Harvest Crusade in 1994. After the music and the message, I knew the Lord was knocking, was on my heart, and wanted me to give up being in control of my life. I got up, walked down to the platform, and asked the Lord to take me out of this garbage and mess, and if He did that, I would do anything He asked. God's Spirit surrounded me and began to melt all of the pain and hurts that I had all of those years, and God's Word started to work in a miraculous way in my life.

He started going to church and learning the Word of God, and now he has gone back to his homeland to start a church and preach the gospel.

What this world can't do, Jesus Christ can!

Jesus delivered the suicidal, tormented, demon-possessed man. So how did the people react? Amazingly, they were afraid (Luke 8:35).

The demonstration of the power of God had frightened them. They should have been rejoicing and praising God, but they were afraid.

You would have thought they would have asked Jesus to stay with them, but they did the opposite: "Then the whole multitude of the surrounding region of the Gadarenes asked Him to depart from them, for they were seized with great fear" (Luke 8:37).

The owners of the swine were angry with Jesus. For some people, after all, Jesus is bad for business. In their case, it was an economic loss. So they decided it would be best for Jesus to go away.

But the fact that Jesus was bad for business wasn't the only reason these Gadarenes wanted Him to leave. More than that, they might have wondered, *If He did that for this one man, would He do the same to us?* They had their own guilt. The presence of Jesus Christ will always produce that reaction.

They could see in His eyes that He knew everything about them. He read them like an open book. They were afraid of what He might do. He might want to bring about change in their lives, and they didn't want to change.

It's important to note that before conversion, there must first come the conviction of sin. Guilt comes before repentance, because it reminds us of our desperate need. But remember that He who causes us to experience that guilt can also remove it.

Yet they told Jesus to go away.

Will you do the same?

And when you get down to it, this sums up the reaction of all humankind to Jesus Christ. It is either "Away with Him!" or "I want to be with Him." We each belong to one of these two groups.

You might protest and say, "I admit that I haven't made a commitment to Christ and said, 'I want to be with Him,' but I have not said, 'Away with Him!' either. I simply haven't decided yet."

But to be undecided is to be against Him. Either we pray for Him to go away, or we pray to allow Him into our lives.

Which is it for you?

Is it "Away with Jesus!" or "Lord, come into my heart"?

Do you know what Jesus did when they told Him to go away? He left. "The entire town came out to meet Jesus, but they begged him to go away and leave them alone. Jesus climbed into a boat and went back across the lake to his own town" (Matt. 8:34–9:1 NLT).

Jesus is a gentleman.

He will not force His way into your life.

He says, "Behold, I stand at the door and knock" (Rev. 3:20). He does not say, "I will kick the door in!"

5

HOW TO KNOW GOD

If you want to know God in a personal way; if you want the assurance that you will go to heaven when you die; if you carry a load of guilt around but you want to be forgiven, here is what you need to do:

> 1. *Realize that you are a sinner.* No matter how good a life we try to live, we still fall miserably short of being a "good person." That's because we're all sinners. We all fall short of God's desire for us to be holy. The Bible says, "No one is righteous—not even one" (Rom. 3:10 NLT). This is because we cannot become who we are supposed to be *without* Jesus Christ.
>
> 2. *Recognize that Jesus Christ died on the cross for you.* The Bible tells us, "But God showed his great love for us by sending Christ to die for us while we were still sinners" (Rom. 5:8 NLT). This is the *good news,*

that God loves us so much that He sent His only Son to die in our place when we least deserved it.

3. *Repent of your sin.* The Bible tells us to "repent therefore and be converted" (Acts 3:19). The word *repent* means "to change our direction in life." Instead of running away from God, we can run toward Him.

4. *Receive Jesus Christ into your life.* Becoming a Christian is not merely believing some creed or going to church on Sundays. Becoming a Christian is allowing Christ Himself to take residence in your life and heart. Jesus said, "Behold, I stand at the door [of your life] and knock. If anyone hears My voice and opens the door, I will come in" (Rev. 3:20).

If you haven't ever invited Jesus Christ into your life, pray a sincere prayer like this one:

Dear Lord Jesus, I know I am a sinner. I believe You died for my sins. Right now, I turn from my sins and open the door of my heart and life. I confess You as my personal Lord and Savior. Thank You for saving me. Amen.

The Bible tells us, "If we confess our sins, He is faithful and just to forgive us our sins and to cleanse us from all unrighteousness" (1 John 1:9).

So if you just prayed that prayer and meant it, then Jesus Christ has now taken residence in your heart! Your decision to follow Jesus Christ means God has forgiven you and that you will spend eternity in heaven. It means you will be ready to meet Christ when He returns.

To help you grow as a Christ-follower, remember to read the Bible, pray, spend time with other Christians by finding a church, and tell others about your faith in Christ. Throughout the rest of this book, we will explore what it means to become a disciple of Jesus Christ, and you'll discover how to share your faith with others. Whether you're a new Christian or someone who has walked with Christ for years, I encourage you to search your heart and read the following chapters carefully.

PART TWO

DISCIPLESHIP

6

ARE YOU HIS DISCIPLE?

*As He passed by, He saw Levi the son of Alphaeus
sitting at the tax office. And He said to him, "Follow
Me." So he arose and followed Him. (Mark 2:14)*

The Christian life is the greatest life there is. Having lived on both
sides of the fence, I can say without a doubt that it is a much better
way to do life. As the Bible says, it's like a turning from "darkness
to light, and from the power of Satan to God" (Acts 26:18).

I wasn't brought up to pray, read the Bible, or go to church.
Growing up, I experienced all the world has to offer, which sent
me on a search that ultimately led me to a relationship with God
through Jesus Christ.

Instead of the turmoil I felt before, I found peace. Instead of
misery, I felt joy. Instead of hate, I had love. Most importantly,
instead of a future separated from God in a place called hell, I now
have the hope of being in His presence forever in heaven.

But the Christian life is more than just praying a prayer and getting "fire insurance," so to speak. The Christian life is following Jesus Christ *as your Lord.* It is following Jesus not only as your friend but as your master.

The problem is this: Many Christians never grow up spiritually. They made an initial commitment to Jesus, but never found out what it means to be a dedicated follower of Christ. In short, they haven't actively pursued what the Bible calls *discipleship.* They still act like spiritual infants.

I have two granddaughters, so of course I think babies are cute. But I also know that babies are a lot of work. For example, teaching a baby how to eat is a long, drawn-out process. When they are first born, babies need to be nursed or fed their formula. After formula, they work up to baby food. When they get their teeth, they can begin eating baby-sized bites of food that have been carefully cut up for them. Later they learn how to use a spoon and fork. Eventually, as children, they learn how to cut, eat, and ultimately, prepare their own food. This is part of growing up.

In the same way, people must grow up spiritually. The Bible warns us, "So let us stop going over the basic teachings about Christ again and again. Let us go on instead and become mature in our understanding" (Heb. 6:1 NLT).

There is a place for teaching and preaching. God has equipped pastors and teachers to build up believers so that "we will no longer be infants, tossed back and forth by the waves, and blown here and there by every wind of teaching and by the cunning and craftiness of men in their deceitful scheming" (Eph. 4:14 NIV). However, once we have learned the basics, we need to grow up spiritually, become mature as believers, and learn how to be true disciples.

Requirements of a Disciple

Early in His earthly ministry, Jesus called out to a tax collector named Levi (Matthew), "Follow Me!" (Mark 2:14). As we learned earlier, "follow Me" may be better translated "follow *with* Me."

In other words, Jesus promises His disciples that He will be a companion and friend as they walk the road with Him. So what criteria must *we* meet, what conditions must be fulfilled to become a disciple of Jesus?

Glad you asked. Jesus actually laid out the requirements of discipleship in Luke 14. He addressed these words to a massive group of people who were beginning to follow Him. Let's set the scene at this time in His ministry.

Immense crowds gathered wherever He went. If you wanted to get near Jesus at that time, you needed as much determination as blind Bartimaeus, who screamed out for Jesus, much to the dismay of the disciples. Or you needed the faith and persistence of the sick woman who reasoned that if she could just touch the Lord in some way, she would be healed.

Clearly, people admired Jesus for His dramatic miracles and insightful teaching. He became enormously popular among the common people, as He elevated the outcasts of society and assured them of God's love, while repeatedly blasting the religious hypocrites of the day.

People admired Him, but they didn't all follow Him. As He looked out on the multitudes, Jesus could see that these people didn't understand what it really meant to be His disciples. So He challenged them. Although His pointed statement was directed to the fascinated crowds, it is still relevant for you and me today:

> If anyone comes to me and does not hate his father and mother, his wife and children, his brothers and sisters—yes, even his own life—he cannot be my disciple. And anyone who does not carry his cross and follow me cannot be my disciple.
>
> Suppose one of you wants to build a tower. Will he not first sit down and estimate the cost to see if he has enough money to complete it? For if he lays the foundation and is not able to finish it, everyone who sees it will ridicule him, saying, "This fellow began to build and was not able to finish."… In the same way, any of you who does not give up everything he has cannot be my disciple. (Luke 14:26–30, 33 NIV)

These were perhaps the most solemn and searching words that ever fell from Jesus' lips. Jesus wasn't calling people to a marginal belief in Him; He called for complete and total commitment. He looked for people whom He could call "disciples." Jesus is still asking us to step out from the crowd, from the fair-weather followers, to become His true disciples.

And why is His call so difficult? Jesus saw a problem developing that we still have with us today: Some people respond only to certain aspects of His message. They pick and choose what appeals to them and pretty much ignore the rest. So Jesus outlined the requirements for following Him, *the true cost of discipleship*. Three times in this short passage, He points out that if you do not do these things, you "cannot be my disciple." So we see that these are absolute prerequisites to true discipleship.

Priorities for a Disciple

Loving God above anyone or anything is the foundation of discipleship. As we just read, Jesus said that anyone who does not hate his father, mother, and even children cannot be His disciple.

A statement like that is *shocking*.

However, as we balance this verse with other passages from Scripture, we know that Jesus isn't commanding the hatred of people, especially not members of our own families. Why would God tell us to honor our fathers and mothers and also demand that we hate them? Jesus even told us to "love [our] enemies" (Matt. 5:44), so we need to grasp the bigger picture here.

Essentially, Jesus says that we should love God more than anyone or anything else—*so much so* that our love for people or things would seem like hatred in comparison.

People have held back from following Jesus out of fear of such a high commitment. People know that if they give their lives to Christ, they will lose a lot of so-called friends. A commitment to Christ might force the end of other relationships. If they give their lives to Christ, their new faith would cause friction in their homes. So people hold back. But Jesus says, "If you really want to be My disciple, you must love Me more than anyone or anything else."

In Luke 9 we read the story of a man Jesus called to follow Him. The man replies, "Lord, let me first go and bury my father" (v. 59). Jesus told him, "Let the dead bury their own dead, but you go and preach the kingdom of God" (v. 60).

It's easy to read this exchange and think, *What is with that?* The guy's father is lying dead, and Jesus says, "Forget about him. He will bury himself. Let's get out of here"?

This isn't what was happening, of course. The man employed a common expression in that culture that meant he wanted to wait until his parents had passed on. In other words, the man was saying, "When it's easier and more convenient, I will do it. Lord, I would like to follow You, but I want to wait until my parents grow old and die. Then, when it fits into my schedule a little better, I will follow You."

We will either find harmony with God and friction with the people in our lives, or we will have harmony with people and friction with God. If we live the way that God wants us to live, then it's going to seriously bother some people. Jesus said, "Woe to you when all men speak well of you, for so did their fathers to the false prophets" (Luke 6:26). If you are truly a follower of Jesus Christ and living in His way, certain people won't like you for that reason alone. Don't be hurt by that rejection. We must understand that this is par for the course. As Jesus said, "'A servant is not greater than his master.' If they persecuted Me, they will also persecute you" (John 15:20).

A true disciple loves God more than anyone or anything else.

The Cross and the Disciple

Jesus underscored the importance of commitment on the part of a disciple when He referred to the cross: "Then [Jesus] said to them all: 'If anyone would come after me, he must deny himself and take up his cross daily and follow me. For whoever wants to save his life will lose it, but whoever loses his life for me will save it'" (Luke 9:23–24 NIV).

Today, we often strip the cross of its original meaning. Shrouded in tradition, it has become symbolic of many things and is used as a religious icon or even an ornate piece of jewelry, studded in diamonds or pearls. Yet the historical cross was a hated, despised symbol—*the symbol of a cruel death.* The Romans reserved this form of torture and execution for the lowest of all criminals.

We wouldn't expect to see many diamond-studded guillotines or electric chairs hanging around people's necks. These machines are symbols of death and shame. The cross is also a symbol of death. When a man carried his cross through the streets of Jerusalem, everyone knew that he was about to die. The convicted criminal would be driven outside the city, nailed to that cross, and placed by the roadside where everyone coming in and out of the city would see him.

So when Jesus spoke those words, "If you want to be My disciple, take up your cross," He chose a despicable symbol of torture and rejection to illustrate what it means to follow Him. The cross symbolizes one thing: *death.* And in the context of a Christ-follower's life, it means dying to self.

Sometimes people identify whatever problem, difficult relationship, or obstacle they face as their "cross to bear." But that's not what "bearing the cross" means. For disciples, it means that they go wherever Jesus directs. Obviously, this isn't an appealing message in our culture. Satan gave an accurate description of humanity when he said, "A man will give all he has for his own life" (Job 2:4 NIV). In other words, when the chips are down, people will give up everything to stay alive, to preserve themselves.

Jesus doesn't advocate what I call "easy-believism." Far too often we hear people say, "Just ask Jesus into your heart. He'll make you a happier person. Let God be your copilot." Some falsely assert that you will become wealthier or healthier once you are a Christian. But that is not the Christianity I read about in the New Testament.

God does not offer Himself to us as some kind of celestial big brother or best buddy. God is absolutely holy and perfect, and we have all sinned horribly against Him. But God, in His great love, bridged the tremendous gap that our sins produced, and He sent His own Son to die on the cross for us. To receive Jesus into our lives, we must not only believe in Him, but we must also turn from our sins, surrender our lives, and follow Him as both our Savior and Lord.

General William Booth, founder of the Salvation Army, wrote of the dangers he saw facing the gospel in the twentieth century. Among other things, he saw a "gospel" that would present "Christianity *without Christ,* forgiveness *without repentance,* salvation *without regeneration,* and Heaven *without Hell"* (emphasis added).[1] And isn't that what we often hear substituted for the true gospel today?

To deny ourselves, take up the cross daily, and follow Jesus Christ flies in the face of the deep self-love that is so prevalent today, even in the church. We hear a great deal about "self-worth," "self-image," and "self-esteem." And this shouldn't surprise us, because the Bible warns us that narcissistic attitudes will be common in the days before Christ's return:

> But mark this: There will be terrible times in the
> last days. People will be *lovers of themselves,* lovers of
> money, boastful, proud, abusive, disobedient to their
> parents, ungrateful, unholy, without love, unforgiving,
> slanderous, without self-control, brutal, not lovers
> of the good, treacherous, rash, conceited, lovers of
> pleasure rather than lovers of God—having a form of
> godliness but denying its power. (2 Tim. 3:1–5 NIV)

What an accurate description of our times! As we look at our nation and see a society coming apart at the seams, we must realize that America's only hope is a nationwide revival.

God gives us His recipe for revival in 2 Chronicles 7:14: "If My people who are called by My name will humble themselves, and pray and seek My face, and turn from their wicked ways, then I will hear from heaven and will forgive their sin and heal their land."

One of the first conditions we must meet in order to have our sins forgiven and our land healed is found in the beginning of this passage: "If My people ... pray." Of the twelve Hebrew words employed to express the single verb *to pray,* the one used here means to "judge self habitually." It doesn't mean to love yourself or to esteem yourself, but to judge yourself ... *habitually.*

This is what Jesus means when He tells us to deny ourselves. Discipleship involves commitment. Although *discipline* is not an appealing word or idea for many of us, it is an essential ingredient to becoming a disciple of Jesus Christ. Discipline requires us to set aside our aims, goals, ambitions, and desires. It involves giving up our wills, dreams, and rights.

Jesus underscored this when He said, "So likewise, whoever of you does not forsake all that he has cannot be My disciple" (Luke 14:33). This does not mean that to live the life of a disciple, one must take a vow of poverty and give everything away. Jesus meant that we are to surrender our claim to our possessions. We are not to be possessed by possessions.

The only "obsession" a disciple should carry is an obsession with Jesus Christ. *He* must be the most important pursuit in our lives. He must be more important than our career or our personal happiness. In fact, we'll never find happiness until we are fully committed to Christ. Happiness is a by-product of knowing Him: "Happy are the people whose God is the LORD" (Ps. 144:15 HCSB).

As Samuel Rutherford said, "The cross of Christ is the sweetest burden that ever I bore."[2] The truth is that when we die to ourselves, *we find ourselves.* When we lay aside personal goals, desires, and ambitions, God will reveal the goals, desires, and ambitions that He has for us. This is what the apostle Paul meant when he said, "I have been crucified with Christ; it is no longer I who live, but Christ lives in me" (Gal. 2:20).

Are you bearing your cross right now and following Jesus? For some people, this may mean suffering persecution. For others, this might require a major change in lifestyle. It may cost you friends. It could even mean dying for your faith. Whatever the case, bearing your cross should influence every aspect of your life.

Until we recognize that everything belongs to Jesus, *we are not His disciples.* If we are aware of God's will for our lives but unwilling to go where God wants us to go, *we are not His disciples.*

From Curious to Committed

In his insightful book on discipleship, J. Dwight Pentecost writes about the idea of radical Christian living, or true discipleship. He sums it up in three simple words: *curious, convinced,* and *committed.*[3]

When Jesus performed His first miracle of turning water into wine, the disciples went from curious to convinced—convinced that Jesus was an extraordinary person, perhaps even the Messiah: "This, the first of his miraculous signs, Jesus performed at Cana in Galilee. He thus revealed his glory, and his disciples put their faith in him" (John 2:11 NIV).

When we first see or hear of Jesus Christ, we are curious. We listen to what He says, learn about His life and miracles, and hear what others say about Him—we are curious like the disciples were when He walked this earth.

But there comes a time when we must step over the line from being curious to *convinced.* I would venture to say that many who attend church today have never crossed that line. They are curious, but nothing more. They are attracted to the message, and maybe even to the Christian life, *but they are still not convinced it is true.*

These people are like the five thousand Jesus fed with only five loaves of bread and two fish. After He performed this miracle, His popularity soared. If you wanted a free meal, follow Jesus of Nazareth. There's no doubt that thousands came to hear Him speak, but surely many came because of their empty stomachs—not their empty hearts. They were interested in Jesus' message as long as it took care of their temporary needs and as long as it was convenient, which becomes clear in their response to His message. After Jesus gave a very difficult series of teachings on commitment and sacrifice, these so-called followers turned away. Then Jesus turned to His disciples and asked if they wanted to leave also.

Peter responded, "Lord, to whom shall we go? You have the words of eternal life. Also we have come to believe and know that You are the Christ, the Son of the living God" (John 6:68–69).

The curious went home, but the convinced stuck with Him. But something more needed to be developed in their belief. They needed to go from being convinced to being committed.

At Caesarea Philippi, Jesus asked the disciples, "Who do people say the Son of Man is?" (Matt. 16:13 NIV), referring to Himself. They replied that many thought Jesus was John the Baptist, while others thought He might be Elijah or Jeremiah.

Then Jesus asked, "But what about you? … Who do you say I am?" (Matt. 16:15 NIV).

Up to this point, the answers He had heard were the answers of the curious. Then a convinced disciple named Simon Peter stood up and made a step toward being committed. He replied, "You are the Christ, the Son of the living God" (Matt. 16:16 NIV). Peter went from being curious and convinced to being totally and completely committed.

Where do you stand? Are you merely curious? Or perhaps even convinced? Have you made that step of faith that is total commitment? You become a disciple in the biblical sense only when you are fully committed to Jesus Christ and His Word.

The Results of Discipleship

John's gospel contains three important verses that will help us understand what it means to be a disciple. They provide us with three evidences, or results, of discipleship.

Result 1: You will bear fruit.

In John 15:8, the cornerstone verse for this chapter, Jesus said, "This is to my Father's glory, that you bear much fruit, showing yourselves to be my disciples" (NIV). If you are a true disciple, then you will bear fruit, and your life will display practical results as you follow Jesus.

Result 2: You will study and obey God's Word.

The second characteristic of a disciple is found in John 8:31, where Jesus said, "If you hold to my teaching, you are really my disciples" (NIV). If you are a true disciple, you will study and obey God's Word. Disciples of Jesus will be students of Scripture and will walk according to its teachings.

Result 3: You will love one another.

A third trademark of a disciple is found in John 13:35. Jesus said, "By this all men will know that you are my disciples, if you love one another" (NIV). As a true disciple, your life will be characterized not only by practical results and a hunger for His teachings in Scripture; you will also love others—especially fellow Christians. Without all of these characteristics, you cannot claim to be His disciple.

Commitment

A true disciple who desires to live a radical Christian life must remain anchored in Romans 12:1: "I beseech you therefore, brethren, by the mercies of God, that you present your bodies a living sacrifice, holy, acceptable to God, which is your reasonable service."

In Jewish wedding ceremonies, the moment at which the father of the bride gives his daughter's hand to the bridegroom is called "the presentation." In the same way, God wants us to *present ourselves* to Him.

In the chapters leading up to this verse in Romans 12, Paul outlines all that God did for us. Paul's idea of discipleship is not simply acknowledging Jesus as God; discipleship according to Paul requires obedience and sacrifice.

Jesus is looking for disciples, not people who will call themselves Christians in name only. He is looking for those who will wholly commit their lives to Him. Jesus has plenty of fair-weather followers today, people who follow Him when it's convenient, when it's socially or economically advantageous, or when they are in the mood. But when a crisis, persecution, or difficulty comes, they throw in the towel and turn away.

Every disciple is a Christian, but not every Christian is necessarily a disciple. Do you want to be more than curious about Jesus—*more than convinced?* Then commit your life to Him, become a disciple, and discover what radical Christian living is all about!

Perhaps a commitment like this seems too difficult. Remember, if God asks you to do something, He will give you the strength to do it. God's calling is also God's enabling. As Philippians 2:13 tells us, "For it is God who works in you to will and to act according to his good purpose" (NIV).

That is our guarantee. God will equip us. Being His disciple doesn't take great knowledge. We don't need great ability. It requires only our availability and our commitment.

However, there are no shortcuts on the road of discipleship. There is no secret I can reveal that will replace years of walking with God and being conformed to His image. We live in an age in which technology makes it possible to get everything quickly. Today we're faced with email, instant messaging, text messaging, Facebook, and

Twitter. Our impatience carries over into our spiritual lives. We're in a rush, so if God wants to communicate something to us, then He had better take advantage of the one opening in our schedule right after lunch. The motto of many Christians today might as well be, "Make it quick, God. Just text me."

But if you really want to be Jesus' disciple, you must radically alter the way you think about your relationship with God.

7

TRAITS OF A DISCIPLE

Now when they saw the boldness of Peter and
John, and perceived that they were uneducated and
untrained men, they marveled. And they realized
that they had been with Jesus. (Acts 4:13)

We need people today who walk and talk with Jesus Christ, people who, before they speak a single word, show that they're different. We need people who, through living godly lives, have earned the right to be heard. We need people who have been with Jesus.

What if you saw someone whose face glowed bright red. You might ask that person, "Were you in the sun recently?" You see the evidence of it in the person's face. In the same way, people need to see the evidence of Christ in our lives.

Would someone look at you and your lifestyle and say, "That person has been with Jesus"? Can people tell that you're a follower of Jesus Christ simply by the way you treat others? By the way you act around your family?

Abiding

As we discussed in the previous chapter, the first result of disciple-ship is that you will bear fruit. But how? We find the answer in John 15:4, where Jesus says quite plainly that we must abide in Him: "Abide in Me, and I in you. As the branch cannot bear fruit of itself, unless it abides in the vine, neither can you, unless you abide in Me."

So what does it mean to abide? It is simply to walk with Him as our Lord and our friend. But it also takes the idea further. To abide means that we sink our roots deep into a love relation-ship with Jesus. It is not walking with Him only when it is easy, convenient, or popular. When we abide in Christ, we remain in fellowship with Him daily, regardless of outward circumstances or inner emotions.

In this verse, Jesus uses the analogy of a vine to describe the importance of abiding in Him. It causes us to think of vegetation that draws its strength from the soil of the earth. If we were to uproot a tree and move it to another area, then after a while uproot it again and move it to a different place, it's quite possible we would damage that tree. And if we repeated the process several more times, the tree would certainly die. Yet that is how many Christians try to live.

Some believers have never found a place of consistency in their walk with God. Often they respond again and again to invitations to receive Christ. They find themselves in a continual cycle of making "commitments" to Christ but quickly fall away when they face the pressures and temptations of the world.

Following his sin with Bathsheba, David said, "Create in me a clean heart, O God, and renew a steadfast spirit within me" (Ps.

51:10). A "steadfast spirit" could also be translated a "consistent" spirit. So to bear fruit, we must consistently sink our roots deep into a relationship with Jesus Christ and walk with Him.

Real spiritual growth comes only through discipline and perseverance. Unfortunately, some in the church often substitute activity for fellowship with God. We see this in an account recorded in Luke 10, after Martha and Mary had invited Jesus to their home for a meal. Martha desperately works to prepare a feast fit for a king, literally, but she whipped herself into a frenzy in the process. We find Martha "distracted with much serving" (v. 40), while Mary, on the other hand, set aside the cares of the world and sat at the feet of Jesus to listen to His every word. Mary is the picture of a disciple who learned the importance of listening, while Martha is the picture of many Christians today.

In our chaotic world, we can easily identify with Martha because we must choose between constant activity and spending time with God. And like Martha, when we fail to sit at the feet of Jesus, we usually end up frustrated.

I have no doubt that Martha's intentions were good; however, she substituted work for worship. There is a time to serve God, but before we can effectively work for Him, we need to learn to wait on Him. Before we can *give* to others, we must *take in* for ourselves. Before we can disciple others, we must learn for ourselves what it means to be a disciple. A disciple will always take time to sit at the feet of Jesus.

This story takes on greater significance when you think of a disciple as a learner, as one who comes to be taught. A disciple is more than a student passively listening to a lecture: The description of Mary conveys the idea that the one teaching possesses full knowledge, and the one listening is doing so intently, marking every inflection of the master's voice with an intense desire to apply the lessons learned.

The attitude of a true disciple would be similar to that of someone on a plane that is about to crash. That person would listen intently as the stewardess gave instructions on how to survive the crash. If I were on that plane, I would listen hard as the flight crew explained how to use a parachute! It is with this attitude that Mary listened to Jesus, and that is how we should listen to Him as well.

God is far more interested in our inspiration than our perspiration. Mary learned the secret of abiding, and we need to learn it as well—if we truly want to be His disciples.

"They Had Been with Jesus"

In the book of Acts, we find a story of the disciples Peter and John, who spent time with Jesus and had been radically impacted by their relationship with Him. As a result, they wanted to tell as many people as possible about Him and their zeal led to their arrest, after which they were brought before the Sanhedrin.

It was a source of amazement to the Sanhedrin, religious leaders themselves, that ordinary fishermen knew and understood the Scriptures so well. They appeared to have more understanding of the Word of God than even the rabbis, the trained professionals. How was this so? Acts 4:13 explains: "And they realized that they had been with Jesus."

These two men were present on the day of Pentecost, when the power of God fell dramatically. A sound like a mighty rushing wind filled the room, and divided flames of fire rested upon the disciples as they waited for this power from on high.

Pentecost had passed and the flames were no longer visible over the heads of the disciples, but they were replaced by burning hearts. So Peter and John, with hearts aflame, headed over to the temple to pray. It was three o'clock in the afternoon on an ordinary day. We don't see an angel instructing them to go to the temple, nor do we read of a pillar of fire going before them and leading them to their destination. It was a day like any other day. They had no idea what God would do.

In the book of Acts, we never see a miracle announced ahead of time. Miracles happened as God chose to perform them. Peter and John didn't put up posters around town that read "Miracle service at the Beautiful Gate! Three o'clock!" But they served God with the gifts He had given them.

As Peter and John made their way to the temple, they passed by the Beautiful Gate where a lame man sat begging. He was probably a fixture outside the temple and may have had his friends strategically position him to be seen by people leaving a prayer service so they might give him a little money. I wonder if people stopped noticing him after a while. Maybe they even stepped over him as they went on their way.

Sometimes we can do the same thing. We can be so indifferent to people around us, so oblivious to the pain in their lives. For the most part, we are preoccupied, chatting away on our cell phones, rushing here and there. As a result, we overlook the needs of people and miss opportunities on our doorstep.

But on this day in Jerusalem, the supernatural invaded the natural. God shook things up a little.

Simon Peter did not in and of himself have the faith to do what he was about to do. God gave Peter a special measure of faith, enabling him to boldly say to the lame man, "Silver and gold I do not have, but what I do have I give you: In the name of Jesus Christ of Nazareth, rise up and walk" (Acts 3:6). And Peter didn't stop there. He took the man's hand and helped him stand to his feet. This was a sink-or-swim moment for Peter. It would either be a great victory or a disaster. Peter went for broke, as he often did.

Once, as Peter watched Jesus walking on the water of the Sea of Galilee, he said, "Lord, if it is You, command me to come to You on the water" (Matt. 14:28). A smile must have appeared on Jesus' face as He told Peter to walk to Him. When Peter swung his legs over the side of the boat and lowered himself onto the water, it supported his full weight. He took one step … and then another … and another. But the wind broke Peter's concentration, and he took his eyes off Jesus. Maybe he also looked over his shoulder to see if the other disciples were watching him. Maybe he looked down at the waves surrounding him. Whatever it was, he faltered. Peter began to sink and cried out, "Lord, save me!" So Jesus pulled him up out of the water.

We tend to focus on Peter's doubting when we read this story, but we should also commend him for walking on the water in the first place! If getting out of the boat had been the wrong thing for him to do, Jesus never would have invited him to do so. Clearly, Peter was willing to take steps of faith.

And here he was, about to take another one. As he pulled the lame man to his feet, "instantly the man's feet and ankles became strong. He jumped to his feet and began to walk. Then he went with them into the temple courts, walking and jumping, and praising God" (Acts 3:7–8 NIV). As people began to realize what had happened, that this was the lame man who begged at the Beautiful Gate, they gathered around the three men. God then led Peter to preach the gospel of Jesus Christ.

This wasn't well received by everyone in the temple. The Sadducees (religious leaders who didn't believe in the resurrection of the dead) had the temple police arrest Peter and John and throw them in jail. The next day, they were brought before the Sanhedrin, which included Annas and Caiaphas, both culpable in the crucifixion of Jesus. They had probably concluded that once Jesus was dead, their problem was over. Ironically, here were Peter and John. They thought they had destroyed the Christian faith by killing Christ, yet they played into the plan and purpose of God.

And Jesus now lived in each of His followers.

This story shows us how God can use ordinary people in extraordinary ways. It is important for us to understand, however, that the miracles we read about in Acts didn't happen every day. The events of Acts occurred over a thirty-year period. Most days were like yours and mine. These Christians would get up every morning and walk by faith, allowing God to lead them. And when people saw disciples like Peter and John, they took note that they had been with Jesus.

Four Marks of an Effective Disciple

Have you been with Jesus? These four elements, the four marks of an effective disciple, caused the early church to turn the world upside down.

1. A person who has been with Jesus will share his or her faith.

A few months earlier, Peter had denied Jesus three times. Now he seemed fearless, speaking with the boldness of Jesus Himself. When you spend time with Jesus, you will become more like Him.

Sometimes when couples have been married for a long time, they begin taking on one another's traits. They finish each other's sentences. They know how their spouse will react to this or to that situation. My wife and I have often joked that, between the two of us, we have one complete brain. When you are around someone a lot, you become more and more like that person.

God's objective in the lives of believers is to make each of us into the image of Jesus Christ. He wants you to become more like Him each day. Romans 8:29 says, "For God knew his people in advance, and he chose them to become like his Son, so that his Son would be the firstborn among many brothers and sisters" (NLT).

The name *Christian* is not one that the followers of Jesus came up with. It was a description given them by their critics—it meant they were like Jesus Christ. A literal translation would be, "They were of the party of Christ."

Are you of the party of Christ? Or are you ashamed to be identified with Jesus? The religious leaders of the first century realized they couldn't stop Christians, because they had been with Jesus. Do people recognize that about you?

2. A person who has been with Jesus will know Scripture.

One thing that got the Sanhedrin's attention was Peter's grasp of Scripture. As you read through his sermon (Acts 3:11–26), note the number of times Peter quotes from various passages of Scripture. This shows us that when you have been with Jesus, you spend time in His Word. The Bible is the autobiography of God. It shows us how to live, how to act, and how to react. If you want to get closer to God, you have to study the Bible, because Jesus said, "Behold, I have come—in the volume of the book it is written of Me—to do Your will, O God" (Heb. 10:7).

You can read the writings or biographies of certain historical figures to learn about them, but God gave us His book, the Bible, so we can learn His story.

3. A person who has been with Jesus will be a person of prayer.

After being released and told not to preach their message, Peter and John joined the other disciples. And what did they do? They held a prayer meeting (Acts 4:29), which gave them even more boldness.

4. A person who has been with Jesus will be persecuted.

Peter and John were arrested. Because we have been with Jesus, we will be treated like Jesus. If everyone likes you, if everyone thinks you are wonderful, if you don't have an enemy anywhere, then something is wrong. Maybe you have thought the opposite. Perhaps you think that Christians should be sweetness and light and that everyone should love you. There is some truth to that. You should be a loving person and a sweet person and a kind person. But you also have to be a godly person and a truthful person and a righteous person. And if you are these things, trust me, that will bother some people. You can tell a lot about a person by his or her enemies and friends. If you walk with Jesus, *you will face persecution.* And if you are a true believer, then persecution will not weaken you, but only strengthen you. If you are not a true believer, then you will abandon what little faith you have.

Then again, sometimes Christians are persecuted because we're obnoxious and unnecessarily offensive. We behave like self-righteous, insensitive fools and wonder why people don't like us. We console ourselves with the thought that we are blessed because we've been persecuted, when all along we were behaving like idiots and we weren't loving people with compassion. The gospel has enough built-in offense. Let's not make it worse. Let's deliver it with compassion.

Jesus said, "Blessed are those who are persecuted for righteousness' sake, for theirs is the kingdom of heaven" (Matt. 5:10). May the persecution you face be a result of your representing Christ, because you are like Christ. If persecution befalls you, that's the best reason.

The Christian life is tough at times. If you think it's all about feeling good and having everything go your way, I promise you won't like being a disciple. Being a follower of Christ is the most joyful, exciting, and challenging life possible. But it is also a life in which you are under the command of someone other than yourself.

Just as soldiers receive and carry out orders from their commanding officer, we must respond to the orders of Jesus Christ. The Bible says, "You therefore must endure hardship as a good soldier of Jesus Christ" (2 Tim. 2:3). Soldiers make a commitment to serve and protect their country, so they respond immediately to the orders they are given. They don't argue with their commanding officer. In the same way, disciples have to make a non-negotiable commitment to serve Jesus Christ. They need to be willing to respond to Him when He leads them. They do what He tells them to do. They go where He tells them to go. They say what He wants them to say. And more and more, they become like Him until the day they see Him face-to-face. So if you don't want to live that way, if it all has to be about you, then you will not make it as a disciple, and you will miss out.

Have you been with Jesus? Today, as you come into contact with
people around you, I hope they can tell that you have been in His
presence. I hope there is an intangible something about the way you
act and the way you speak that prompts them to wonder what's different about you.

While there's a place for words in preaching the gospel, it is also
a glorious thing when we earn the right to be heard by the way that
we live, and someone says to us, "There is something special about
you. There is something different about you, and I want to know
more about what you believe. *Please tell me.*"

You never know what opportunities will open up for you each
day. That's why every Christian always needs to be ready to respond
to the leading of the Lord, just as Peter did. We are told in Scripture,
"Be ready in season and out of season" (2 Tim. 4:2). Or, as another
translation puts it, "Be prepared, whether the time is favorable or
not" (2 Tim. 4:2 NLT).

May God help us to be like the first-century believers and turn
our world upside down in the midst of persecution, challenges, and
temptations.

May people see that we have been with Jesus.

8

THE COST OF DISCIPLESHIP

And being in Bethany at the house of Simon the leper,
as He sat at the table, a woman came having an alabaster
flask of very costly oil of spikenard. Then she broke
the flask and poured it on His head. (Mark 14:3)

One of the reasons the Christians of the first century turned their world upside down was their sense of total and complete abandon. God would say to Peter, "Reach down, take that lame man's hand, and pull him to his feet," and he would do it. God would tell Philip, "Go to the desert," and he would go (see Acts 8:26–27). The disciples took risks.

In committing to be a disciple you must consider the cost. Obedience to God's plan of discipleship is costly. Too often, a would-be disciple desires God's best but fails to pay the price necessary. How can we be willing to give so little to the One who gave so much for us? He gave everything to us, and frankly, He expects nothing less in return.

Yet many believers are like the farmer who was known for his stinginess. When his cow gave birth to two calves, he looked at them and said, "Lord, I'm so thankful for this blessing that I'm going to give You one of my calves." He told his wife of his decision, which surprised her in light of his normally selfish ways.

When she asked him which calf he was planning to give to the Lord, he replied, "I'm not sure yet."

As time went by, one of the calves became sick. A few days later, the farmer came out of the barn, the lifeless calf in his arms, and sorrowfully announced, "Honey, I've got bad news. The Lord's calf just died."

Likewise, some Christians give God what they no longer want. But that is not the attitude we need to have. How we miss out! How we misunderstand! God doesn't want our leftovers. He deserves our very best. He has given so much to us that we should want to give everything we have back to Him.

"She Did What She Could"

We see the act of generous giving modeled by Mary—the same Mary who sat at the feet of Jesus while Martha hurried to prepare a meal for Him. In another account, we see her offering Jesus the most precious thing she owned. In fact, she did something so outstanding and so significant that Jesus said, "Assuredly, I say to you, wherever this gospel is preached in the whole world, what this woman has done will also be told as a memorial to her" (Mark 14:9).

At this point in the life and ministry of Jesus, He had already had a number of confrontational exchanges with the religious leaders. They wanted Him dead, plain and simple. But by this time Jerusalem was overflowing with pilgrims who had arrived for the Passover celebration. Jesus had thousands of followers, and the religious leaders were afraid that if they arrested and killed Him, His followers would revolt.

So while the forces of darkness amassed to do their wicked work, Jesus decided to share a meal with friends and followers at the house of Simon the leper. Presumably this was Simon the *healed* leper. Lazarus, the man who had been resurrected from the dead, and his sisters Martha and Mary attended, along with the apostles. I would have loved to eavesdrop on the conversations that took place that evening. Jesus had just delivered the Olivet Discourse, which was His overview of the coming events. Some probably asked follow-up questions. Maybe someone turned to Lazarus and said, "What was it like to die and come back again? Tell us more."

At some point during this visit with Jesus, Mary took some special and costly perfume, broke open the flask, and poured it on the head of Jesus. The perfume was called spikenard, presumably imported from India. Most likely it was a family heirloom and worth a lot of money. It would have been one thing to sprinkle a few drops on Him, which was culturally acceptable. But Mary wanted to do something outstanding, something extravagant to show her love for Jesus, so she poured the whole bottle on Him.

Not everyone appreciated her sacrifice: "Some of those present were saying indignantly to one another, 'Why this waste of perfume? It could have been sold for more than a year's wages and the money given to the poor.' And they rebuked her harshly" (Mark 14:4–5 NIV).

In other words, was such an extravagant gesture really necessary? Was that an act of good stewardship? Was that the right thing to do?

This response is typical of so many Christians today. Like dutiful Pharisees, they will give only what is required by God. They ask questions like, "Can I do this and still be a Christian?" In essence, they openly seek to give the bare minimum to God. Sure, they will pray briefly before a meal or before going to sleep—*if they remember.* They read the Bible—if they can make time in their busy schedules. They give something to the Lord—if they have a little spare change in their pockets. They sing worship songs in church—as long as the worship leaders don't get carried away.

So what was the inspiration behind this display of abandon and sacrifice in Mary? It was Jesus Himself. She thought that nothing was too good for the Lord. And what could be wrong with that?

Jesus both defended and commended Mary for her sacrificial act: "Why are you bothering her? She has done a beautiful thing to me. The poor you will always have with you, and you can help them any time you want. But you will not always have me. She did what she could. She poured perfume on my body beforehand to prepare for my burial" (Mark 14:6–8 NIV).

If we, like Mary, know anything of what God has done for us, then we will feel compelled to do more for Him. Nothing is ever wasted when it is done for the glory of God. You can't do everything, but you can do *something.* You can't win all of the people in the world to Christ, but you can win *some people.* Shouldn't we seek to give Him the finest that we have to offer? Doesn't Jesus deserve our best?

One day your life will come to an end. I assure you of this: You will not regret going to church too much. You will not regret reading the Bible too much. You will not regret sharing your faith.

What you will regret is that you didn't do these things *more*.

Selling Out for So Little

The Bible makes it clear that we are not our own. We have been bought with a price, and therefore we are to glorify God with everything we are (1 Cor. 6:19–20). We must recognize that our lives belong to Him, that our time is His time, and that our resources and possessions are His resources and possessions. We must consider this cost when we commit to life as a disciple.

I heard about a remarkable method that hunters use to catch monkeys in Africa. They take a coconut and cut a little hole large enough for a monkey to squeeze its hand into, but not large enough for it to pull its fist out. Next, they hollow out the coconut, put some warm rice inside, and place them under trees where their nets are hanging.

Then the hunters wait.

When the monkeys smell the rice, they reach inside the coconuts. But the hunters have learned that the monkeys will not open their fists to let go of the rice, and therefore cannot get the coconut off. When the monkeys start banging the coconuts on the ground in frustration, the hunters arrive and easily capture them. Even as the monkeys see the nets, they still won't let go of the coconuts, because they want the rice. As a result, they are trapped.

Many people live their whole lives for a handful of rice: a handful of possessions … a handful of pursuits … a handful of pleasures.

They give up what God could do in their lives in exchange for fleeting, temporal things. Like Esau, they sell everything for a bowl of stew (Gen. 25:29–34).

True discipleship takes sacrifice. In Luke 9 we find a passage that illustrates the extent of a disciple's commitment:

> As they were walking along the road, a man said to
> him, "I will follow you wherever you go."
>   Jesus replied, "Foxes have holes and birds of the
> air have nests, but the Son of Man has no place to
> lay his head." (Luke 9:57–58 NIV)

In modern language, Jesus said, "Look, buddy, I'm not headed to the Jerusalem Ritz-Carlton Hotel. You might want to reconsider. Mine is a life of difficulty and sacrifice. Do you know where I'm going? Ultimately I'm going to die on a cross. Is that where you want to go? Consider what you're saying!"

We must give this man some credit, though. He felt inspired. He saw Jesus, admired Him, and immediately blurted out that he wanted to follow Him. He seemed to have a good heart, but he was impulsive. He had not counted the cost. He did not know what was ahead. Jesus made it clear that if this man wanted to be a disciple, he would have to forsake all that he had. It's no different for us. We must have the same attitude of detachment to anyone or anything that would prevent us from fully following Him.

A few verses later, Jesus states, "No one who puts his hand to the plow and looks back is fit for service in the kingdom of God"

(Luke 9:62 NIV). This is a stern warning for those who live a life of second-guessing, questioning their commitment.

What (or Who) Is Holding You Back?

Discipleship requires not only *giving* our best but also *giving up* anything that hinders us in our commitment to follow Christ. Hebrews 12:1–2 tells us,

> Therefore, since we are surrounded by such a great cloud of witnesses, let us throw off everything that hinders and the sin that so easily entangles, and let us run with perseverance the race marked out for us. Let us fix our eyes on Jesus, the author and perfecter of our faith, who for the joy set before him endured the cross, scorning its shame, and sat down at the right hand of the throne of God. (NIV)

As we seek to walk with Christ, sometimes we travel with too much weight. We drag things along that shouldn't be in our lives. It might be something we do that slows us down, or it might be someone with whom we spend time. Whatever it is, we need to get rid of excess weight.

Whenever my friend Franklin Graham visits, he wants to go for a run. He will say, "Come on, Greg. Let's go for a run in the morning!"

"Okay," I say. "Looking forward to that."

Franklin is a good runner. He is disciplined. He can run consistently for forty-five minutes, sometimes an hour. I, on the other hand, am good for about four minutes. Then I get tired. So we start running. As I start to slow down, Franklin will say, "Greg, come on! Greg! Greg, run!" So I will run a little bit more.

"I am just going to walk," I will tell him after a while.

"Come on! Run!" he says.

"I am running," I tell him. *"In my heart I am running with you!"*

I think Franklin realizes that I slow him down. He is trying to run a race, and I am impeding his performance.

We have people in our lives who can have the same effect on us spiritually. When we're around them, they slow us down, because they don't have the same commitment to the things of God.

We'll say to them, "Hey, let's go to church today!"

And they'll reply, "Oh, I don't know. It's raining. It is so dangerous to drive in the rain. Do you want to go to the mall instead?"

They drag us down, and we know it.

The Bible tells the story of Abraham and his nephew Lot. Lot was not committed to walking with God like his uncle. And whenever Lot was around, he seemed to drag Abraham down. God even told Abraham to leave Lot, but he refused for a time. Yet it wasn't until Abraham unloaded Lot that God began to speak to him and bless him again.

We all know people like that who slow us down spiritually. That is why Paul advised Timothy, "Run from anything that stimulates youthful lusts. Instead, pursue righteous living, faithfulness, love, and peace. Enjoy the companionship of those who call on the Lord with pure hearts" (2 Tim. 2:22 NLT). Spend time with people who share the commitment to discipleship that you have.

Understand the Terms

To count the cost is to understand the terms of the commitment. So how much are you willing to give?

In our journey to become disciples, we make decisions every day that will either encourage or discourage our spiritual growth. When we get up in the morning, we can either watch the news or read the Bible. On the weekend, we can either sleep in or go to church. In dealing with others, we can either harbor a grudge or choose to forgive. When thinking about the future, we can either worry or pray. With each choice, we will either regress or progress, retreat or advance in our quest to be His true disciples.

If you look back at this point in your life and have regrets, know that you can't change the past. But you can change *what you do today* and *what you will do tomorrow.* You can change your course!

Is your commitment to discipleship like that of the farmer who determined it was "the Lord's calf" that had died? Or, are you willing to pay the price and commit to radical Christian living?

Every hour, every minute you give to serve Jesus is not wasted. Every resource you have invested is not wasted. Every thought you give to His Word is not wasted. Rather, these are the best possible investments.

9

DISCIPLESHIP AND THE BIBLE

*Then Jesus said to those Jews who believed
Him, "If you abide in My word, you are
My disciples indeed." (John 8:31)*

It always amazes me to see how much care and cultivation it takes
to make flowers grow. My wife loves to plant flowers. She can spend
hours pulling weeds, driving out snails, and amending the soil. This
hard work is necessary for flowers to grow. Yet how quickly and easily
weeds can sprout up and take over! A weed can bloom in the middle
of a street or through a crack in the sidewalk, without any caretaker
or special watering. But delicate, vulnerable flowers require constant
attention.

This is a classic illustration of the contrast between a believer's
new nature and old nature. If we want to be closer to Christ and live
a life that is pleasing to Him, we need to cultivate and nurture our
new nature. The moment we stop strengthening and building our

new nature is the moment the old one comes back to haunt us—like a weed growing up through concrete. It takes very little encouragement for our old nature to cause us trouble. All we need to do is neglect the new nature. As the apostle Paul wrote, "I say then: Walk in the Spirit, and you shall not fulfill the lust of the flesh" (Gal. 5:16). There are disciplines every believer must maintain if he wants to live the Christian life as God intended.

The Key to Spiritual Progress

In this chapter, we'll examine the first of these disciplines found in John 8:31, in which Jesus says, "If you hold to my teaching, you are really my disciples" (NIV). If you and I want to truly be disciples of Jesus Christ, we must learn and hold to the Word of God.

By most measures, success or failure in the Christian life depends on how much of God's Word we get into our hearts and minds on a regular basis and how well we obey it. The Bible teaches everything we need to know about God. If we neglect the study of Scripture, then our spiritual life will ultimately fall into disrepair.

President Abraham Lincoln once said of the Bible, "It is the best gift which God has ever given man. All the good from the Savior of the world is communicated to us through this Book. But for that Book we could not know right from wrong. All those things desirable to man are contained in it."[1]

Honest Abe was exactly right.

The Bible is the most amazing document ever given to man. Technically speaking, it is not one book but sixty-six books written over 1,600 years by kings and peasants, philosophers and fishermen, poets and statesmen. Each of the writers was inspired by God to write down His Word. They were not the authors; God was. *He breathed each word.*

Why is it, then, that so many believers fail to open their Bibles? Could it be that many Christians simply lack a spiritual hunger for the truth?

One way for a doctor to know whether a person is healthy is to check his or her appetite. If a person lacks an appetite, it usually means something is wrong. In the same way, when a Christian doesn't have an appetite for the Word of God, something is probably wrong. Some Christians see reading God's Word as a duty, a bit of drudgery, even an obligation. But that changes when they see the difference the Word makes in their daily lives.

Hungry Christians are healthy Christians. The Bible tells us, "Like newborn babies, crave pure spiritual milk, so that by it you may grow up in your salvation, now that you have tasted that the Lord is good" (1 Peter 2:2–3 NIV). To desire the pure milk of the Word means that we intensely want to grow. If we are not making spiritual progress, then it is possible we're not hungry enough for the Word.

The prophet Hosea's cry is still relevant: "My people are destroyed for lack of knowledge" (Hos. 4:6). Today, many believers throw in the towel, fall into sin, or are misled by false teachings because they haven't developed the discipline of studying the Bible. If we are to be disciples of Jesus Christ, leading effective and successful Christian lives, then we must make God's Word a priority.

Proverbs 2:1–9 provides a wonderful series of promises that will help us get the most from our study of Scripture. For every promise, there is a condition that we must fulfill. The conditions listed in the first five verses state that we must receive His words, treasure His commandments, cry out for discernment, and seek understanding as though we were mining for gold.

Treasure My Commands and Know for Yourself

Let's examine the first of these principles for getting the most out of Scripture, which we find in Proverbs 2:1, 5: "My son, if you receive my words, and treasure my commands within you … then you will understand the fear of the LORD and find the knowledge of God." So to get the most out of Scripture, we must both *receive it* and *treasure it*.

Referring to the Christians in Berea, Acts 17:11 says, "Now the Bereans were of more noble character than the Thessalonians, for they received the message with great eagerness and examined the Scriptures every day to see if what Paul said was true" (NIV). The Bereans checked the accuracy of Paul's teaching against Scripture. If they examined the apostle's teaching, then how much more should we be checking the teaching of our own pastors and teachers against Scripture? It sounds as if the Bereans are both *receiving* the Word and *treasuring* the Word, doesn't it?

Some people today claim to speak for God, but if anyone questions the validity of their teachings, usually the questioner is rebuked for daring to challenge those who claim to be modern apostles or prophets. What foolishness! No person is above being questioned. If people scrutinized the words of the apostle Paul according to Scripture, then how much more should we scrutinize those who often seem to contradict Scripture!

Along with their search of Scripture, the Bereans received Paul's message with "all readiness of mind" (Acts 17:11 KJV). This was not simply eagerness on the part of these believers to learn something new but a deeper willingness to reinforce and apply what they already knew.

It's a sad fact that many Christians think they know more than they actually do. Often seemingly mature believers have nothing more to offer than a blank stare when faced with a question concerning a basic biblical doctrine. They know what they are supposed to believe, but they are unable to defend it biblically. They believe something only because they have been told that it's true.

This is very dangerous. Our faith shouldn't hinge on what someone tells us, no matter how credible and godly the person. If that person says something that is incorrect, our faith could be shattered. We must base our faith solely on God's Word. We need to know the truth for ourselves.

Discerning Bible Study

The Bible tells us to "Be diligent to present yourself approved to God, a worker who does not need to be ashamed, rightly dividing the word of truth" (2 Tim. 2:15). The phrase *rightly dividing* means "dissecting correctly" the word of truth.

Do you believe that Jesus Christ is God? Do you believe that Jesus Christ is the only way to get to the Father? Do you believe that God has a plan for your life and wants to reveal His will for you? If so, can you back your beliefs biblically? These are essential Christian doctrines. Unfortunately, many Christians can't answer these questions with intelligent, scriptural responses.

One reason for this is that often we do not read the Bible intelligently. Many times we read, but we fail to understand *what* is being said in the larger context. We have no idea *who* is speaking, nor do we know the circumstances surrounding the passage.

For instance, if you read about various animal sacrifices in the Old Testament, you might become confused if you didn't have a basic understanding of the New Testament. If it were me, I might conclude that the best way to approach God is to sacrifice an animal. However, with an understanding of the New Testament, I realize that the sacrificial system foreshadowed what Jesus would do on the cross and is no longer necessary.

Here are some key questions you might ask yourself as you open the Bible and study a passage of Scripture:

> What is the main subject of the passage?
> Who are the people revealed in the passage?
> Who is speaking?
> About whom is the passage speaking?
> What is the key verse?
> What does it teach me about Jesus?

As you read, it is also important to ask how the text might apply to your daily life. When reading a passage, also ask yourself these questions:

> Is there a sin mentioned that I need to confess or forsake?
> Is there a command given that I should obey?
> Is there a promise made that I can look to in my current circumstances?
> Is there a prayer given that I could pray?

As you read, stop and think about what God may be showing you. It's good to chew your spiritual food. That's what it means to meditate on Scripture. We are better off reading five verses slowly and understanding what they mean than reading five chapters quickly and not getting anything out of them. Learn to slow down. Learn to allow the Holy Spirit to speak to you through each passage as you read.

Psalm 1 shows us an example of a person who has learned to walk with God and tells us that "his delight is in the law of the LORD, and on his law he meditates day and night" (v. 2 NIV). As disciples, we should do the same.

This brings us to another important ingredient in learning from Scripture, which we find in Proverbs 2:3: "Cry out for insight, and ask for understanding" (NLT). To get the most out of studying the Bible, we need to pray for understanding. We need to come before the Lord and pray something like this:

> Father, I believe You are the author of this Book. I believe, as You say in your Word, that all Scripture is breathed by You. Therefore I am asking You, as the author, to take me on a guided tour. Help me to understand, and show me how these truths apply to my life.

That form of sincere prayer will cause the Bible to come alive in your study times. The Bible also tells us that to know God, we should seek Him and His wisdom as though we were "mining for gold" or searching for treasures (see Prov. 2:4).

As believers in the United States, we rarely recognize what a treasure the Bible is. Recently, I was talking with a Bible publisher who told me of a growing trend in America today in which consumers are more interested in how a Bible coordinates with their outfit than the type of study features it might contain. We have been spoiled in so many ways. Many of us have more than one Bible at home. In fact, I own Bibles in different sizes, shapes, colors, and translations.

But in China and other countries where the Bible is restricted, even prohibited, this Book is a great treasure. I've heard stories of churches in China that have had only one Bible for an entire congregation. They take that Bible, tear out pages, and give them to individual members of the congregation to memorize. For many of these underground Christians, Bibles are as valuable as gold—*even more so.* We need to see that same value in God's Word and not take it for granted. As Psalm 19:9–10 says, "The laws of the LORD are true; each one is fair. They are more desirable than gold, even the finest gold" (NLT).

When you're reading through the Bible, think about it as though you were mining for gold. Have you ever dropped a quarter? Do you look for a quarter if you drop it? I do. Do you look for a dime? I do. Do you look for a penny? I do, depending on the circumstances.

Let's say that you somehow misplaced one million dollars. Do you think you would search for it? If I'm willing to look for a quarter, then I would definitely look for a million dollars.

My point is that there is buried gold in the pages of Scripture. You need to get into it, search for it, and find all the treasure that's in the Bible for you.

Why Memorize?

The best way for me to remember things is to write them down. When I write something down, that particular thing is engraved more deeply in my memory, much deeper than if I had only read it once. I might not even have to refer to what I wrote down later, but I will likely still remember it.

It is a good practice to keep a journal or notebook with your Bible. When you study the Scriptures and a passage speaks to you, write down whatever God shows you. Maybe that nugget of thought won't be useful to you in that moment, but the next day, or even a month later, it may be just what you need.

Once a verse or passage of Scripture is ingrained in your memory, it will always be there to use or draw on. Undoubtedly, there will be times when the verse you memorized pays great dividends. It may bring comfort to your heart or strength in a time of intense temptation. The psalmist wrote, "I have hidden your word in my heart, that I might not sin against you" (Ps. 119:11 NLT). Although it is good to carry a Bible in your briefcase, backpack, or purse, by far the best place to carry God's Word is in your heart.

God tells us, "Fix these words of mine in your hearts and minds; tie them as symbols on your hands and bind them on your foreheads. Teach them to your children, talking about them when you sit at home and when you walk along the road, when you lie down and when you get up" (Deut. 11:18–19 NIV).

Colossians 3:16 says, "Let the word of Christ dwell in you richly." That verse could be translated, "Let the word of Christ permeate your life," or, "Let the word of Christ be at home inside of you." In other words, allow yourself to fall in love with the Word of God. You will never regret it.

What you will regret is all the time you spent watching television. You will regret all the time you spent surfing the Web. But you will never regret a single minute you spent studying the Bible or memorizing its verses.

Applying What We Learn

It is not enough to study the Bible on a daily basis or even memorize it; its teachings must affect the way we live. It is not enough to go through the Word of God; the Word of God must go through us. It is not important how we mark up our Bibles, it's how our Bibles mark us.

Remember, Jesus said that if we continue in His Word, then we are His disciples (John 8:31). The word *continue* is the same word Jesus used in John 15:7 when He spoke of "remaining in Him," or in some translations, "abiding." He said, "If you remain in me and my words remain in you, ask whatever you wish, and it will be given you" (NIV).

We abide in Jesus as we draw strength from Him. In the same way that a vine draws its resources from the soil and a branch draws its resources from the vine, we are to maintain unbroken fellowship, communion, and friendship with God. If we are abiding in God's Word, it means we are drawing our ideas, thinking, and lifestyle from its teaching. Consequently, our actions and speech will change.

Is God's Word affecting you today? Is it sustaining your life? Is God's Word guiding your thoughts, the way you conduct your business, your home life, and even your free time? If not, then you cannot be called His disciple. We become disciples when we put ourselves under the authority of His Word and submit to its teaching.

Which Type of Hearer Are You?

In Luke 8 we find a story called the parable of the sower, which illustrates the common obstacles to God's Word taking root in our lives. The seed represents God's Word, while the soil represents the different types of people who receive it.

The first mentioned in this story is the one I call the *highway hearer:* "A farmer went out to sow his seed. As he was scattering the seed, some fell along the path; it was trampled on, and the birds of the air ate it up" (Luke 8:5 NIV). The seed never takes root with highway hearers. They hear God's Word, but they don't believe it. It is not as though they embrace it or say they want to believe. The highway hearers are not interested. They are not open-minded, and they aren't seekers.

Next is the *rocky road hearer:* "Some fell on rock, and when it came up, the plants withered because they had no moisture" (Luke 8:6 NIV). In contrast to the indifference of the highway hearers, the rocky road hearers embrace the message. They say, "Yes! This is it! This is what I have been searching for!" But a week later, they just walk away. They say, "I'm not into that anymore." They didn't have the endurance required in their walk with God to bear any fruit.

This brings us to the *thorny hearer:* "Other seed fell among thorns, which grew up with it and choked the plants" (Luke 8:7 NIV). This third type of hearer represents a gradual process that could last months, even years. Just as a weed doesn't burst out of the ground, grab a plant, and shake it violently, this choking is a gradual process that kills off a particular kind of spiritual growth. It starts out subtly: like going to church less often or reading the Bible less. Spiritual priorities move down while other priorities move up—until growth comes to a standstill.

Last, we have the *fruitful hearer:* "But others [seeds] fell on good ground, sprang up, and yielded a crop a hundredfold" (Luke 8:8).

Why does this person bear fruit? Because he or she wants to bear fruit. Good ground is made that way by the work of the Master Gardener with our cooperation. You don't naturally have a receptive heart. *You make it receptive.* Stumps need to be uprooted. Weeds must be pulled and burned so new seed can be planted.

God works in the soil of the human heart. We don't like it when He comes along and removes something that we've allowed to take root in our lives, such as a boulder of sin, a weed of rebellion, or a stump of disobedience. God says, "We've got to get this stuff out of here so we have fertile and receptive soil for the Word, and then the fruit will grow."

God wants His Word to permeate every area of your life—your home, your business, your leisure time, and your prayers. Learning, knowing, and spending time in God's Word is a necessity for all who want to be His disciples.

10

DISCIPLESHIP AND PRAYER

Once Jesus was in a certain place praying. As he finished, one of his disciples came to him and said, "Lord, teach us to pray, just as John taught his disciples." (Luke 11:1 NLT)

Prayer should be second nature to every Christian, almost like breathing. But sadly, prayer is greatly lacking in the lives of many believers.

A disciple must be a person of prayer, because prayer is one of the essentials of discipleship. It's the key to having passion and power in our witness for Jesus Christ.

When Job encountered his many trials, he cried out, "If only there were someone to arbitrate between us, to lay his hand upon us both" (Job 9:33 NIV). Job couldn't find anyone to reason or argue for him, to stand in the gap for him before God. He felt as though he couldn't get through to God.

Perhaps you've felt this way. Maybe sometimes it seems as if God isn't really listening to you. But if you have received Jesus Christ as your Lord and Savior, this should not be the case, because Jesus opened the way for us to stand boldly at the throne of grace to find help in time of need (Heb. 4:16). The Bible tells us that Jesus lives to intercede for us (Heb. 7:25). So today we can approach God through Jesus, our Mediator: "For there is one God and one mediator between God and men, the man Christ Jesus" (1 Tim. 2:5 NIV).

The great value of prayer is that it keeps us in touch with God. And believe it or not, God wants you to get to know Him through prayer. He wants to reveal Himself to you. We might expect God to give us all we need for every situation all at once. That's simply not the way it is. In fact, that would be dangerous.

God has a lot to give us, but He gives it to us as we need it. And the discipline of prayer brings us into dependence on God as He works in our lives.

In Matthew 6, we find Jesus dealing with several common misconceptions people have regarding prayer. The first misconception concerns our motives. Jesus said, "And when you pray, do not be like the hypocrites, for they love to pray standing in the synagogues and on the street corners to be seen by men. I tell you the truth, they have received their reward in full" (Matt. 6:5 NIV).

The problem with the religious people of Jesus' day, the Pharisees, was that they prayed to impress others. On street corners and in the marketplace they lifted up their hands and prayed in an ostentatious manner. Others would walk by and think, *Just look at that man of God. He loves God so much that he can't even wait to get to the synagogue to pray!*

What they didn't realize was that for the person praying it was an issue of pride. Perhaps he was thinking, *What a man of God I am.*

Everyone is looking at me. Everyone is impressed with my spirituality. I am so holy.

This attitude will result in a prayer unheard by God. A person so concerned with what others think about him is too full of himself to be effective in his prayer. He is like the self-righteous Pharisee Jesus mentioned who "prayed about himself" (Luke 18:11 NIV). God won't hear the prayer of a pride-filled person, because it's nothing less than sin. The Bible tells us that if we regard iniquity in our hearts, the Lord will not hear us (Ps. 66:18). So make no mistake—spiritual pride is as much a sin as lying, stealing, or any other kind of immorality, even though it's subtler.

The next misconception Jesus addressed was *how* the Pharisees were praying: "And when you pray, do not keep on babbling like pagans, for they think they will be heard because of their many words" (Matt. 6:7 NIV). The Pharisees repeated ritualized prayers over and over again. They seemed to believe that the longer the prayer, the more spiritual and pleasing to God it was.

But God is not interested in eloquence. Prayer should come from the heart. He isn't interested in how perfect our prayers sound, whether they rhyme, or how long they last. He's only concerned with how genuine the prayer is. One of the most eloquent prayers found in Scripture comes from a man who said, "God, be merciful to me a sinner!" (Luke 18:13). *That is an effective prayer.* This man was honest with God. He said what he was thinking and simply laid it out before the Lord. Sometimes we feel so concerned with technique that we miss the point.

When Jesus used the word *pray,* He used a word that literally means to "wish forward." To "wish" describes a desire or a hope of our heart. "Forward" implies action. Prayer is the idea of wishing for something from the depth of our hearts and bringing that desire forward to the throne of God. Often our mouths and minds can go through some ritualized prayer, while our hearts never engage.

Sometimes people wonder about the best posture for prayer. Is it okay to pray with your eyes open? Yes, you can pray with your eyes open. Leaving your eyes open doesn't somehow cancel out your prayer. But I think it's a good thing to close your eyes when you pray, because this helps you to concentrate. Also, you can pray on your knees, or you can pray sitting down, or even lying down. You can even pray while you are driving—just be sure to keep your eyes open in that case.

The Bible tells us about people praying in all sorts of unusual places. They prayed in prison. They prayed on mountaintops. They prayed in valleys. One man even prayed from the belly of a whale, and *God heard his prayer*. Wherever you are, you can pray.

Another common misconception Jesus unmasked was the *true purpose* of prayer. He said, "Your Father knows what you need before you ask him" (Matt. 6:8 NIV). God already knows our needs. Therefore, prayer isn't a way of instructing or informing God. Nor is it somehow bending the will of God. Some people think they can influence God or move Him a certain way through prayer. Nothing could be further from the truth. Prayer is laying hold of God's willingness. Prayer is not pushing our will into heaven; prayer is getting God's will down to earth.

Martin Luther said, "By our praying ... we are instructing ourselves more than Him."[1]

"Teach Us to Pray"

"Lord, teach us to pray" (Luke 11:1 NIV). This was the request one of the disciples brought before Jesus after watching Him in prayer. Sometimes Jesus would stay up all night in the presence of His heavenly Father and pray. While the disciples slept, Jesus would pray. In the garden of Gethsemane, shortly before His arrest, He told Peter, "Watch and pray, lest you enter into temptation. The spirit indeed is willing, but the flesh is weak" (Matt. 26:41).

In response to the disciple's request, Jesus gave us a template for prayer that we call the *Lord's Prayer*. A more accurate name for it might be the *Disciple's Prayer,* because it is for us to pray, not for Him. Jesus never needed to pray the words, "And forgive us our debts, as we forgive our debtors" (Matt. 6:12). He was sinless. This was a prayer for His disciples, and for us. And because this section is about discipleship, it is fitting that we develop a clearer understanding of this prayer.

Within the Lord's Prayer, Jesus gives us the principles we need to understand how to communicate with God. Remember, the disciples watched Jesus pray. They saw Him spend time with His Father. They saw His intimacy and closeness with God. In contrast, they had also seen the ritualized, cold, and academic prayers of the religious hypocrites.

So Jesus began His lesson on prayer by saying, "This, then, is how you should pray" (Matt. 6:9 NIV). Let me emphasize that Jesus was not giving the disciples a canned, formalized prayer. In fact, this prayer is never repeated in the New Testament. That's not to say that it's wrong to pray this prayer verbatim or to use it as an act of worship to God. But we should not adhere to it merely as a ritual.

There is nothing magical in simply uttering the words. However, we can learn from its form, content, and structure how to pray more effectively. It is a model and pattern for all who pray.

The Lord's Prayer is divided into two sections. The first three petitions focus on the glory of God, while the last three deal with our needs as humans.

"Our Father in Heaven"

When we pray, we should first recognize the object of our prayer: "Our Father in heaven" (Matt. 6:9 NIV). It's good to pause before you pray and realize that you are addressing the Creator of the universe. Too often we rush into the presence of God and absentmindedly rattle off our petitions. First, we ought to be quiet and wait before the Lord, even before we say a word. After a time of contemplating Him, we can then more reverently pray, "Our Father."

Those words should remind us that He is our Father, the One who has our best interests at heart. As 1 John 3:1 reminds us, "Behold what manner of love the Father has bestowed on us, that we should be called children of God!" From this we can be assured that whatever happens as a result, our prayer falls in accordance with what our Father wants for us. We may not always agree with what He decides, but we can know that His will for us is good. We can know that He loves us with an everlasting love.

When you've been around a little while, you gain the advantage of twenty-twenty hindsight. You can look back on your life and see how God's wisdom prevailed. I can think of things that I prayed for years ago, things that I was certain were the will of God for me, and He said no. However, some of those prayers were answered some time later. Other prayers God didn't answer in the way I had hoped. But now I can look back and say, "Lord, thank You for the way that You worked in my life."

We need to trust that our Father in heaven is doing the same for us right now. Psalm 84:11 says, "No good thing will He withhold from those who walk uprightly." Just because God says no doesn't mean that He's turning His back on us. It means that He's looking out for our welfare.

When we pray to our Father in heaven, it should remind us that He is the Creator. This fact should fill our hearts with humility and awe. Uttering those words helps to prepare our hearts and to see our smallness in light of His greatness.

"Hallowed Be Your Name"

Following our acknowledgment of our loving Father and Creator, Jesus reminds us of His holiness: "Hallowed be Your name" (Matt. 6:9). The word *hallowed* could also be translated "sanctified," "revered," or "holy." Saying these words is a recognition that we need to be sanctified or set apart for Jesus Christ in order to live holy lives. Because He is holy, we also should be holy. All of our ambitions, interests, and pursuits should reveal that we follow a holy God.

A powerful prayer must first seek God's glory. When you read through the Scriptures, the great prayers recorded in the Bible always glorify God and set Him apart. For example, read Elijah's prayer on Mount Carmel (1 Kings 18:36–37).

The privilege of prayer was not given to us so that we could demand things from God. James 4:3 tells us why some of our prayers go unanswered: "When you ask, you do not receive, because you ask with wrong motives, that you may spend what you get on your pleasures" (NIV). We should ask only for the things God wants to give us. If He gave us everything we asked for, these gifts would ultimately destroy us. We must seek His glory above our own desires.

I have found that when I seek God's glory, His will, and His kingdom, He blesses me. It's not wrong to ask for what we believe is necessary, but I make it a point to preface my petitions with something like, "Lord, I think this would be a great thing for You to do, but Your will be done. If I'm missing something, if there's more to this than I know, then overrule my petition. I know whatever You do will be best."

This is one way to pray with His glory in mind.

"Your Kingdom Come"

The next phrases in the Lord's Prayer are *Your kingdom come. Your will be done on earth as it is in heaven* (Matt. 6:10). A person cannot pray, "Your kingdom come" until he or she first prays, "My kingdom go."

All too often, our prayers are meant to establish our kingdoms. We want to be the captains of our own ships, the masters of our own destinies. This will not do if we truly want His kingdom and if we truly want to be His disciples. We must turn over the reins completely to Him.

Therefore, it is essential that we learn what the will of God is, so that we can pray for it. If you pray according to the will of God, your prayers will always be answered in the affirmative. According to 1 John 5:14–15, "This is the confidence we have in approaching

God: that if we ask anything according to his will, he hears us. And if we know that he hears us—whatever we ask—we know that we have what we asked of him" (NIV).

As we spend time in the Word, learning the will of God and the desires of God, our prayers will change. They will shift from self-centered or self-indulgent and orient toward the glory and will of God. As we align ourselves with His will and start praying for it, we will begin to see the results. I believe most prayers are not answered because they are outside the will of God.

Once we have discovered God's will, we can then pray aggressively and confidently for it to come to pass. We can pray, believing it will happen, because we know it's not something we've dreamed up on our own. James 1:6–7 tells us that when we pray, we should "be sure that [our] faith is in God alone. Do not waver, for a person with divided loyalty is as unsettled as a wave of the sea that is blown and tossed by the wind. Such people should not expect to receive anything from the Lord" (NLT).

When Jesus went to His hometown, we are told that "He did not do many miracles there because of their lack of faith" (Matt. 13:58 NIV). In other words, unbelief, or a lack of faith, will cancel out our prayers. *Therefore, we must pray, believing.*

So where do we get such faith? "Faith comes by hearing, and hearing by the word of God" (Rom. 10:17). I can pray, believing that God will save a person's soul, because I am told in Scripture that God is "not willing that any should perish but that all should come to repentance" (2 Peter 3:9). So I can pray in full confidence, believing and hoping that God will save that individual. Nevertheless, the ultimate result is God's doing and not my praying.

I can also pray with biblical authority for revival in our country, city, home, or church. I believe this is something God wants to do, because as we have seen, it is clearly proclaimed in Scripture (2 Chron. 7:14). And on a more personal level, I can pray authoritatively that God would make me more like Jesus and that He would reveal His will to me (see Rom. 8:29; 12:2).

"Give Us This Day Our Daily Bread"

After establishing to whom we are speaking, giving Him glory and acknowledging His rightful position, we then come to the first petition: "Give us this day our daily bread" (Matt. 6:11).

Let me once again emphasize the order of Jesus' model prayer. Before we utter a word of personal petition, Jesus shows us that we must first realize that God is our audience, then hallow His name, and ask for His will above our own.

You see, God is not our heavenly butler.

In this first petition, notice that Jesus doesn't say, "Give us this *year* our *yearly* bread" or even, "Give us this *month* our *monthly* bread." God wants us to rely on Him *daily!* Most people in our increasingly independent society do not *want* to depend on God; they would rather depend on themselves.

It is also noteworthy that in John 6, Jesus described Himself as the Bread of Life. We must seek a fresh encounter each day with Him. Yesterday's "bread" is largely useless for today, much like the manna God provided to the children of Israel during their wilderness wanderings. The manna would not keep overnight without spoiling; it was good for that day only. This principle applies to our spiritual lives as well. God wants to give you fresh direction each day. Scripture tells us, "Because of the LORD's great love we are not consumed, for his compassions never fail. They are new every morning; great is your faithfulness" (Lam. 3:22–23 NIV).

"Forgive Us Our Debts"

We find the next petition in Matthew 6:12: "Forgive us our debts, as we also have forgiven our debtors" (NIV).

A true disciple recognizes the need for confession of sin and forgiveness—the Bible says that unconfessed sin will hinder our prayers (Ps. 66:18). If we cling to sin in our lives, God will not hear us. We should always remember to ask God to forgive our sins, even those we do not recall or recognize as sin. After all, the only sin God cannot forgive is the one we will not confess.

Some people misunderstand the second part of this phrase: *as we forgive our debtors.* They teach that the condition of being forgiven is that we must first forgive others. I do not believe this, because it is a clear contradiction to other teachings in Scripture. The only way we can receive forgiveness from God is to ask for it: "If we confess our sins, he is faithful and just and will forgive us our sins and purify us from all unrighteousness" (1 John 1:9 NIV).

Clearly God does not make forgiving others a prerequisite, necessarily, for finding forgiveness ourselves. What He says here is this: "If you have really been forgiven and you understand something of that forgiveness, then you will also forgive other people." If you do not forgive others, then I question whether you know anything of God's forgiveness in your own life.

Essentially, a forgiven person will be a forgiving person. A true disciple will harbor no grudges toward others. The true disciple knows it will hinder his or her prayer life and walk with God. Let's not forget what Jesus said: "By this all men will know that you are my disciples, if you love one another" (John 13:35 NIV).

For that reason, no child of God can walk around holding bitterness, anger, or hostility in his or her heart toward another person without feeling the conviction of sin. We must forgive others as we have been forgiven.

"Do Not Lead Us into Temptation"

Jesus concludes the Lord's Prayer with, "And do not lead us into temptation, but deliver us from the evil one. For Yours is the kingdom and the power and the glory forever. Amen" (Matt. 6:13). The "evil one" is a reference to Satan. We are to recognize our total weakness apart from God and the fact that we are engaged in a spiritual battle. We need our Father's protection. Without Him, we are completely vulnerable. We must depend on Him for daily bread, depend on His will for direction, and depend on Him for power.

ACTS

The Lord's Prayer is the model, the template for prayer that Jesus gave us. First, we must recognize the awesomeness of God. Before saying a word, worship, adore, and thank Him for all He has done. Confess your sins, and forgive those who have wronged you. Pray for His will in your life and the rule of His kingdom in your heart and the hearts of others. Then, having put things in their proper perspective, bring your needs before Him.

Another way to remember the structure of this model prayer is to use the simple acronym, ACTS:

Adoration

Confession

Thanksgiving

Supplication

First, I adore God and praise Him.

Then, I confess my sin.

Next, I remember to give thanks.

Finally, I offer my supplications.

With this model prayer as our guide, we must not fail to "pray without ceasing" (1 Thess. 5:17). As we pray, these essential ingredients of effective prayer will help us make great strides in growing as disciples of Jesus.

11

DISCIPLESHIP AND
THE CHURCH

And the Lord added to the church daily
those who were being saved. (Acts 2:47)

So far, we've looked at two essential ingredients for our growth as disciples of Jesus Christ: Bible study and prayer.

The third essential involves the significance of a church and community in the life of the disciple. I cannot stress enough the importance of regular fellowship and participation in a Bible-believing church. As we come into the church and find our place in it, we are then in a position to give to others what God has given to us. Every Christian has an important role in the body of Christ, and God has given special gifts to each one.

The emphasis, of course, is not merely on what a believer receives from the church but on what he or she can contribute. The Bible tells us to "think of ways to motivate one another to acts of love and good works. And let us not neglect our meeting together, as some people do, but encourage one another, especially now that the day of his return is drawing near" (Heb. 10:24–25 NLT).

The church is not only a place where we can learn God's Word and worship Him; it is also somewhere we can be equipped for service.

A healthy church will be filled with believers who desire not only to receive but also to give. Rather than having an attitude that says, "Bless me; do something for me," a healthy church will want to help others. It will follow the example of Jesus, who came not to be served but to serve (Matt. 20:28).

That is not to say we don't need to be ministered to and spiritually nourished when we go to church, for indeed we do. The number-one priority in selecting a church should not be how close it is to your home or how nice its facilities are. The most important question must be, "Is this church teaching God's Word?" I don't just mean topical Bible studies but biblical exposition in which you work your way through books of the Bible. There is a place for addressing topics, but everything ought to be done from a biblical perspective. People should bring their Bibles to church and read from them in the service. The pastor should preach from the Bible as well.

But as we take in teaching, we should also recognize our privilege and responsibility to serve. If a need or opportunity arises, we should be willing to leave our nice comfortable seats and volunteer. The attitude of a truly thankful Christian is, "God has given to me, and as a result, I want to give to others."

The Function of Spiritual Gifts

God gave gifts to each of us who have put our faith in Jesus Christ, and He has also empowered us with His Holy Spirit. Are you using and cultivating the gifts God gave you? The Bible specifically tells us that as believers, we are to use our spiritual gifts as we await the return of Christ (1 Cor. 1:7).

Also, failing to discover and use the gifts God has given us could cause us to quench the Holy Spirit, which the Bible specifically commands us not to do (1 Thess. 5:19). The word *quench* communicates the idea of extinguishing something. So when God's Spirit nudges us to say or do a certain thing and we refuse, we quench or extinguish the Spirit.

Some Christians express negative feelings toward the gifts of the Spirit, probably because there's so much abuse in this area. Often those who claim to be using the gifts of the Spirit are some of the strangest people around. As a result, some Christians conclude that if these are the gifts of the Holy Spirit, they don't want anything to do with them.

But let's not look at the gifts that way. Let's take a step back and look at them in a balanced, biblical way. I believe in the power of the Holy Spirit, but I believe it is a practical power that God wants us to have in our lives, the same power that caused the early church to turn the world upside down.

Ephesians 4, a definitive chapter on the gifts of the Spirit, explains why God has given them to us: "It was he who gave some to be apostles, some to be prophets, some to be evangelists, and some to be pastors and teachers, to prepare God's people for works of service, so that the body of Christ may be built up" (Eph. 4:11–12 NIV).

First, we see that God gave us the gifts of the Spirit for the perfecting or the maturing of the body of Christ. God raised up pastor-teachers, evangelists, and prophets to help us grow up, so "that we should no longer be children, tossed to and fro and carried about with every wind of doctrine, by the trickery of men, in the cunning craftiness of deceitful plotting, but, speaking the truth in love, may grow up in all things into Him who is the head—Christ" (Eph. 4:14–15). God gave us these gifts, working through people like pastor-teachers, so we will be equipped and will mature.

Second, God gave us the gifts of the Spirit so we can do all He called us to do in the church. God gave each of us a gift, or gifts, for us to use to bless others. The gifts of the Spirit are not a hobby to play with; they are tools with which to build and weapons with which to fight.

Third, God gave us the gifts of the Spirit to bring unity to the church, "till we all come to the unity of the faith and of the knowledge of the Son of God, to a perfect man, to the measure of the stature of the fullness of Christ" (Eph. 4:13). As we use these gifts, we discover that no one person has all the spiritual gifts. God, in His sovereign will, gave certain gifts to certain people. As Romans 12:4–6 reminds us, "Just as each of us has one body with many members, and these members do not all have the same function, so in Christ we who are many form one body, and each member belongs to all the others. We have different gifts, according to the grace given us" (NIV).

· Fourth, God gave us the gifts of the Spirit for the growth of Christians spiritually and for the growth of the church numerically: "From him the whole body, joined and held together by every supporting ligament, grows and builds itself up in love, as each part does its work" (Eph. 4:16 NIV). When a church is grounded in God's Word and energized by the Holy Spirit, it will reach out, not satisfied to keep to itself. It will permeate, challenge, and confront our culture.

Many people have become passive spectators in the church, charter members of the "Bless Me Club." This mentality causes spiritual stagnation. God did not intend for us to take in without ever giving anything out.

Secrets of the Early Church

To better understand how we should function as disciples in the body of Christ, let's look at how Jesus established the New Testament church. Acts 2 records the first day in the life of this early church. Here we find the first-century disciples in action. We also find principles that make for an effective church and establish the true disciples' place in such a community.

At first glance, this text reveals that the early church was dramatically different from much of the church today. What was normal to them is radical to us. We see pretty quickly that discipleship is "radical Christian living." Normal Christian living in the New Testament was a passionate, Spirit-empowered, all-consuming devotion to God and His Word.

We must remember that the Holy Spirit launched the early church. To be effective Christians, we must also depend on the power of the Holy Spirit. When we become Christians, the Holy Spirit takes up residence inside of us. The Spirit is there to guide us into truth. He is there to assure us that we are children of God.

Another dimension of power is available to us as believers. Jesus said to His disciples, "But you shall receive power when the Holy Spirit has come upon you; and you shall be witnesses to Me in Jerusalem, and in all Judea and Samaria, and to the end of the earth" (Acts 1:8). The word Jesus used here for "upon" is different from words used elsewhere when speaking of the Spirit living inside of us. This "upon" experience empowers us with the boldness we need to live the Christian life. It is the power to live a consistent life, the power to be bold enough to share your faith.

The early church began in the power of the Holy Spirit and continued that way. If we want to flourish and be effective in our witness for Jesus Christ, then we must begin in the power of the Spirit and depend on that power until our last day.

"They Continued Steadfastly"

In Acts 2:42, we find the key reason for the early disciples' effectiveness: "And they continued steadfastly in the apostles' doctrine and fellowship, in the breaking of bread, and in prayers." The early Christians had an intense passion for participating in the life of the church, but more importantly, they demonstrated consistency and passion, or *steadfastness*. These two ingredients helped them do God's will.

Also, the early believers did not take for granted the privilege of meeting together. The more I travel, the more thankful I am for what God is doing in America and in American churches. Pastors in Eastern Europe have told me how hard it is to do what God wants them to do with the restrictions imposed by government. Pastors in Ethiopia have told me how they and members of their congregations have been tortured and imprisoned for preaching the gospel and following Jesus. Those of us in the West are privileged to have the freedoms we do, but many times, we take these freedoms for granted. We must remember to pray for our brothers and sisters who live in countries without religious freedom.

What is your attitude toward going to church? When you go to church, do you go with an earnest hunger for the spiritual sustenance of God's Word (1 Peter 2:2)? Do you crave it? That passion and hunger can make a difference. The early believers' passion was directed toward the "apostles' doctrine," and because of that passion, the early church continued in God's Word. As disciples, we must do the same.

The early believers' passion was also directed toward fellowship. We have somehow lost the true meaning of that word. Often we hear it used in church gatherings, where we are promised "food, fun, and fellowship." But is that what the early church experienced? What is fellowship, exactly?

First of all, fellowship is not merely Christian social activity. Though it may involve that to some extent, true fellowship encompasses a greater commitment. The word used for fellowship in the New Testament is a very distinct Greek word: *koinonia*. It also can be translated "communion," "partnership," "contribution," or "distribution." Each of these words provides a different facet of *koinonia*.

In part, fellowship is a common link with another individual that includes friendship, spiritual intimacy, unity, and a partnership in doing the work of Christ here on earth.

The word *communion* speaks of friendship and intimacy. God wants us to have friendship and intimacy not only with Him but also with one another. This special bond of communion can bring

Christians even closer together than family. Two believers share a unique exchange as God's Spirit works in their lives.

The word *partnership* implies cooperation. Fellowship is not only mystical communion; it is also a practical relationship. Fellowship as partnership involves helping and working with another person, as well as praying for and worshipping with him or her.

Finally, we look at the words *contribution* and *distribution*. These also imply practical help for fellow believers through the sharing of food, clothing, and other resources. The Bible tells us that if we see brothers and sisters in need and fail to help them, then we are without faith (James 2:15–17). When confronted with such a situation, we need to obey God and help our fellow Christians. This too is part of fellowship. We see this element of fellowship clearly at work in the early church as we read that "they shared everything they had" (Acts 4:32 NIV).

God delights when His people gather together for *koinonia*. In fact, God promised to manifest Himself uniquely at these times. The psalmist wrote that God inhabits the praises of Israel (Ps. 22:3 KJV). When in community, we set our eyes and hearts above our circumstances and focus on our Father, it brings everything else into perspective. God's presence can be uniquely sensed at those times.

God will even manifest Himself in a special way in our conversations with other Christians. Malachi 3:16 tells us, "Then those who feared the LORD talked with each other, and the LORD listened and heard. A scroll of remembrance was written in his presence concerning those who feared the LORD and honored his name" (NIV). In its original Hebrew, the phrase *the LORD listened and heard* means "to prick the ear; to bend down so as not to miss a word."

In essence, God says in this passage, "When My people come together and speak of Me, it pricks My ear. It causes Me to come down and listen carefully so as to not miss a word." That should be both exciting and frightening. Maybe you've heard it said that Jesus is the unseen listener of every conversation. *Think about that.* When Jesus hears us mention His name to fellow Christians, it's as though He says, "They're talking about Me. I want to hear." And as if that weren't enough, there's a scroll of remembrance, written in His presence, containing the names of all those who fear the Lord and honor His name in true biblical fellowship.

Along with fellowship, the early Christians also "continued steadfastly" in prayers (Acts 2:42). The word *prayer* here could also be translated "steadfast earnestness." As I pointed out in the last chapter, prayer is a key element in being a disciple of Jesus. But it is also a primary element of an effective church. And the Bible characterizes the early church as steadfast in prayer.

"Gladness and Simplicity of Heart"

The Bible talks about how the first-century disciples had "gladness and simplicity of heart" in their fellowship (Acts 2:46). Do you feel glad when it is time to go to church? David wrote, "I was glad when they said to me, 'Let us go into the house of the LORD'" (Ps. 122:1). These days some people say, "I was *mad* when they said to me, 'Let us go into the house of the Lord'"!

When addressing His disciples in the Sermon on the Mount, Jesus said, "The eye is the lamp of the body. If your eyes are good, your whole body will be full of light. But if your eyes are bad, your whole body will be full of darkness. If then the light within you is darkness, how great is that darkness!" (Matt. 6:22–23 NIV). If we are set apart for God and for His singular purpose, we will seek Him first, and our lives will be full of light. On the other hand, if we have double vision, we may look to God, but we will also look to the world—and our body will be full of darkness. When we try to pursue what both God and the world have to offer, our lives will exhibit fear and confusion.

In addition, if we allow ourselves to be consistently influenced by the things of this world, this can dull our appetite for God's Word and pull us away from Him. It can also lessen our interest in prayer, and our desire to be with God's people.

However, when we live as disciples, we look forward to going to church where meeting with other believers will be like a spiritual oasis where we can be refreshed. It will be an occasion to encourage one another as we go out to live in this world as witnesses for Jesus Christ.

Finally, we read that "the Lord added to the church daily those who were being saved" (Acts 2:47). A healthy church is a growing church. Likewise, a healthy believer is one who will shine light in this world of darkness. Even as the Lord adds to the church daily, a disciple of Jesus will be an instrument of God, drawing people to Christ.

Our Future Reward

One day, you will stand before God, and He will reward you for your faithfulness. He will not overlook even the smallest, most insignificant gesture on behalf of His kingdom. Jesus said that our service to God, even if it is not seen by people, is seen by Him: "Your Father who sees in secret will Himself reward you openly" (Matt.

6:4). Speaking of this day in the future, the Bible also says, "For we must all appear before the judgment seat of Christ, that each one may receive what is due him for the things done while in the body, whether good or bad" (2 Cor. 5:10 NIV).

This is not to be confused with the great white throne of judgment (Rev. 20), at which anyone whose name isn't written in the Book of Life will be cast into the lake of fire. This great white throne of judgment is only for the nonbeliever.

We find more about the judgment seat of Christ (the Bema Seat judgment), exclusively for believers, in 1 Corinthians:

> For no one can lay any foundation other than the one we already have—Jesus Christ.
>
> Anyone who builds on that foundation may use a variety of materials—gold, silver, jewels, wood, hay, or straw. But on the judgment day, fire will reveal what kind of work each builder has done. The fire will show if a person's work has any value. If the work survives, that builder will receive a reward. (1 Cor. 3:11–14 NLT)

According to this and other passages in Scripture, our *presence* in the kingdom is guaranteed by the promises of God, but our *position* in the kingdom will be won or lost by the quality of service we render here and now. Salvation is a gift to us because we have put our faith in Jesus. But honor is a reward for service to Jesus.

There's nothing wrong with having a career and making a living. But if that career becomes more important in your life than

God, you will have a problem. If your possessions, a hobby, or a ministry become more important than God, know that the fire will go through those things at the judgment seat of Christ and nothing will be left to show for your life.

One day, God will ask what you did with the gifts and talents He gave you. Everyone has been given certain skills and talents, and therefore, we all have something to bring in the service of God.

Yet many times we don't use our gifts for His glory. Instead, we chase after our own desires in life. The Bible teaches that we were put on this earth to bring glory to God. *That is why we are here.* God says, "everyone who is called by my name, whom I created for my glory, whom I formed and made" (Isaiah 43:7 NIV).

Let's mark it well in our minds and hearts: Our purpose is to glorify Him in all that we do with our lives.

12

DISCIPLING OTHERS

It is not that we think we are qualified to do
anything on our own. Our qualification comes
from God. He has enabled us to be ministers
of his new covenant. (2 Cor. 3:5–6 NLT)

This is the most important chapter on discipleship in this book. This
is what I have been building toward in this section, because now we
come to the practical result of being a disciple of Jesus Christ: *passing
on what we have learned and discipling others.*

Prior to His ascension, Jesus gave His disciples these marching
orders:

All authority in heaven and on earth has been
given to me. Therefore go and make disciples of all
nations, baptizing them in the name of the Father
and of the Son and of the Holy Spirit, and teaching

them to obey everything I have commanded you.
And surely I am with you always, to the very end of
the age. (Matt. 28:18–20 NIV)

To feel the impact of these commands on our lives as His disciples, we must make two important observations.

First, the three verses you just read are often referred to as the Great Commission. Notice that it is a *commission* as opposed to a *suggestion*. Jesus never *suggested* that we should carry the gospel to the world. It was—*and is*—a command.

Second, these words weren't directed only to the original twelve disciples, nor are they meant exclusively for pastors, evangelists, and missionaries. These commands are for every follower and disciple of Jesus Christ. Since I am His disciple, then I am commanded to go and make disciples of others. And if I am not making disciples of others, then I am not really being the disciple He wants me to be.

What, then, does it mean to make disciples? Verse 20 defines it as "teaching them to obey everything I have commanded you." Simply put, it's not only sharing our faith with others but also living out our faith so that people can observe it in action.

With this understanding, we now have a proper basis for examining in greater detail what it means to make disciples.

Empowered for the Task

God will give the power to do whatever He asks of us. The calling of God is also the enabling of God (2 Cor. 3:4–6). Since He commanded us to go and make disciples, then we can be confident He will be there to give us the ability to see the task through to its completion.

Notice Jesus' words in the Great Commission: "All authority has been given to Me in heaven and on earth. Go therefore and make disciples." Since Jesus Christ has all authority and if He is living inside us, then His power is at our disposal to accomplish the task before us.

Still, to accomplish this task, we all need a strong dose of boldness from the Holy Spirit. In Acts 4:23–31, we see an interesting display of boldness in the lives of Peter and John. As I pointed out earlier, they had been preaching the gospel, which infuriated the religious leaders. As a result, the leaders arrested them and forbid them ever to preach again. Peter and John couldn't comply with that, however, so they prayed,

> Now, Lord, look on their threats, and grant to Your
> servants that with all boldness they may speak Your
> word, by stretching out Your hand to heal, and that
> signs and wonders may be done through the name
> of Your holy Servant Jesus. (Acts 4:29–30)

After they prayed, the Bible tells us that the place where they were meeting was shaken, and they were filled with the Holy Spirit and spoke the word of God boldly.

Here Peter and John were in trouble for their outspokenness, so what did they do? They prayed for even greater boldness. They had laid hold of Jesus' promise to them in Acts 1:8: "But you will receive power when the Holy Spirit comes on you; and you will be my witnesses in Jerusalem, and in all Judea and Samaria, and to the ends of the earth" (NIV). Most of us suddenly become "chickenhearted" when it comes to sharing the gospel. We need to ask God for the power He has already made available to us.

The hardest thing about sharing your faith is getting started and forcing those first words out of your mouth. In this moment, the power of the Holy Spirit is essential. Once the ball is rolling, you will discover that sharing your faith can become a joy and a blessing to you. Better yet, you may play an important role in changing someone's eternal destiny.

The Salt of the Earth

In the gospel of Luke, Jesus concluded His own definition of discipleship by saying, "Salt is good, but if it loses its saltiness, how can it be made salty again?" (Luke 14:34 NIV). To receive the full benefit of what Jesus was saying, we need to understand the first-century mind-set. In Roman culture, salt was very important. Next to the sun, salt was the most important thing there was. Roman soldiers were sometimes paid in salt, which is where the expression "He's not worth his salt" originated. With this in mind, Jesus is saying, "You are to be salt in this earth. You are valuable. You can make a difference."

A distinct quality of salt is that it transforms everything with which it comes into contact. For instance, just a little pinch of salt in a glass of water changes the taste of the entire glass. In the same way, even one faithful Christian in an ungodly situation can make a difference.

Salt also stimulates thirst. When you buy popcorn at the movie theater, you quickly discover that it has been heavily salted, probably with the intent of stimulating your thirst so you will buy a drink at the concession stand.

Like salt, we can stimulate spiritual thirst in others if we live godly lives. If non-Christians see something different in you, that you're not like everyone else and that you live a life directed by certain spiritual principles, they can find it very appealing. When people see a Christian maintain a sense of calm while facing difficult circumstances, it can make them curious about our faith. Remember, our lives are the only Bible some people will ever read. Christians are to be living epistles, written by God and read by men (2 Cor. 3:2).

One of the greatest compliments paid to a Christian is when a non-Christian says, "What is different about you? There's a quality that I admire, and I want to know more. Tell me about what you believe." That is the result of being salt.

Jesus called us to be fishers of men, and one thing that is helpful in fulfilling that role is to first throw out the bait. If I want to start a conversation with the person next to me on a plane, I will often pull out my Bible and set it on the tray. Some people look at me as though I have a highly contagious disease, and they want to quickly move. But others will ask what I'm reading. This often opens the door to share God's truth.

When sharing your faith with someone, it's generally a good idea to talk about how God is working in your own life. Give people an opportunity, and if they respond, tell them a little more about Jesus. If their interest continues to grow, explain what it means to know Christ, what Christ did, and how we should respond to Him.

Sometimes the conversation will come to a point where someone doesn't want to hear any more. If that's the case, don't push it. As 2 Timothy 2:24–25 says,

And the Lord's servant must not quarrel; instead, he
must be kind to everyone, able to teach, not resentful.
Those who oppose him he must gently instruct,
in the hope that God will grant them repentance
leading them to a knowledge of the truth. (NIV)

As I finish talking with someone, I often recommend reading
the gospel of John, because it was written so that we may believe
that Jesus was the Son of God (John 20:31). In the future, maybe a
resistant person will start the conversation again.

The Bible says we are to be "as shrewd as snakes and as innocent
as doves" (Matt. 10:16 NIV). We must act with wisdom without
being overly aggressive. Some Christians try to stuff the gospel down
people's throats, which almost never works. Others argue and use
pressure tactics to coerce a person into the kingdom of God. I sup-
pose they feel the end justifies the means. But keep this in mind:
If people can be argued into believing, they can be argued out of
believing. If they can be pressured in, they can be pressured out. Our
responsibility as Christians is simply to proclaim the truth of the
gospel and leave the conversion process to God.

The Light of the World

Jesus used two analogies to show the impact Christians should have
in this world: *salt* and *light*. In contrast to being salt, which signifies
living what you believe, being light signifies *proclaiming* what you
believe.

Jesus said, "Let your light so shine before men, that they may see
your good works and glorify your Father in heaven" (Matt. 5:16).

Too many believers try to be light without also being salt. They talk the Christian talk, but they don't walk the Christian walk. Quite honestly, it would be better if they didn't say a thing since they do not back it up with their lifestyle.

In contrast, there are those who are salt without being light. They live godly lives, but they don't tell people *why;* they don't proclaim their faith. We must find the balance. Romans 10:14 says, "How then shall they call on Him in whom they have not believed? And how shall they believe in Him of whom they have not heard? And how shall they hear without a preacher?" God wants us to be instruments through which He can speak.

There is a right way and a wrong way to share the gospel message. Therefore, it is important to rely on Jesus and let Him guide us. I believe that God wants us to be sharpshooters, not machine gunners. I have seen machine-gun evangelists who gauge their success by how many people they can talk to in one hour. If you do this instead of really taking time with someone, your talk may not have any real or lasting effect. It may even drive people away.

I have found that the most effective sharing takes time. It's far better to sit down for an hour and talk genuinely with one person than to rattle off clichés to scores of people. Some of the most profound things Jesus ever said were in one-on-one conversations. His talks with the Samaritan woman (John 4:5–42) and with Nicodemus (John 3:1–21) are our examples for evangelism today. Jesus spent time with these individuals, so how much more should we take time for conversations with others?

We must let God's Holy Spirit lead as we share our faith. Remember, when a person comes to Christ, it will always be a result of God's work, not our own. Jesus said, "No one can come to Me unless it has been granted to him by My Father" (John 6:65). No brilliant human argument will ever win over another person. Conversion begins with the work of the Holy Spirit, and it must happen in God's timing. We always need to be ready, because we never know when we will be called into action.

True Discipleship

The full concept of discipleship includes sharing our faith, leading people to Christ, and helping them to mature in their faith. But somewhere along the line, the church has separated evangelism from discipleship. However, there is no such distinction in Scripture. We shouldn't just pray with people and send them on their way. Rather, our call as disciples extends to helping new believers grow spiritually and become dedicated, fruitful, and mature disciples of Jesus Christ. Then we trust those believers will repeat the process with someone else. *And so the cycle continues.*

After Saul's conversion, there was great doubt among the believers about whether he had come to genuine faith in Christ. You see, Saul was one of the primary persecutors of the early church. He actually approved of the first execution of a Christian recorded in the New Testament, a young man named Stephen.

So upon hearing that the notorious Saul had become a believer, naturally, the disciples were afraid it was just a ploy to find out where they met so he could turn them over to the authorities. But God spoke to a man named Ananias and told him to go and visit Saul. Ananias obeyed, found Saul (who later changed his name to Paul), and took the time to pray for him and encourage him (Acts 9:10–19).

In addition to Ananias, God brought a man named Barnabas into Paul's life. Barnabas introduced Paul to the disciples and personally reassured them that his conversion was sincere.

This is a good illustration of how true discipleship can happen. Discipling someone is not just teaching; it's also being a friend to that person. Sadly, many people who accept Christ fall through the cracks because no one helps them get established in the faith. It can be difficult for these people to make friends in the church.

New believers may come to a church for the first time and be encouraged, but when the Bible study starts and they hear something like, "Turn to Matthew chapter five," they immediately feel lost because they don't have the faintest idea where to look.

That's exactly how I felt when I started going to church. I didn't understand the language of the Christians. They had their own unique vocabulary—sometimes we call it *Christianese*. I thank God that a man took me under his wing. He invited me back to church and introduced me to his Christian friends. After the services, he explained what different phrases meant and answered all my questions.

In Acts 18, we find the story of Aquila and Priscilla, who exemplify how we should help new converts. They saw a young man named Apollos who was filled with enthusiasm for the things of God. However, he needed more insight into what he was learning. Aquila and Priscilla took him into their home and "explained to him the way of God more adequately" (Acts 18:26 NIV). As a result, after spending time with them, Apollos was encouraged and became even more effective in what God called him to do.

When we lead someone to Christ or meet new Christians, we must take the initiative to see that they get stabilized in their newfound faith. Take them to church with you, introduce them to your friends, and most importantly, *be a friend.*

New believers not only need to hear the truth; they need to see it lived out. They can't get that from a pulpit on Sunday morning. They need to see it in the lifestyle of a person in day-to-day living. Obviously, they will have questions: How does a Christian act at work? How does a Christian behave when she drives? How does a Christian treat his wife and children? How does a Christian spend her free time? What movies can a Christian see? These questions and more are a part of the discipleship process.

A mature believer can be a model for applying the truths of God. As Colossians 1:28 says, "We proclaim him, admonishing and teaching everyone with all wisdom, so that we may present everyone perfect in Christ" (NIV).

The Bible offers numerous examples of this process. With young Timothy, the apostle Paul repeated the discipleship process he went through. In the Old Testament, Elijah discipled Elisha. Moses discipled Joshua. And most notably, Jesus discipled His apostles. In speaking of this process, Paul said in 1 Thessalonians 2:11–12, "For you know that we dealt with each of you as a father deals with his own children, encouraging, comforting and urging you to live lives worthy of God" (NIV).

One thing that keeps Christians from being active disciples is the fear of not having sufficient Bible knowledge. News flash: It's not necessary to be a Bible scholar to lead others to Christ and disciple them. Remember, no matter how much you don't know, you probably know a lot more than a new Christian does. Begin by sharing the building blocks of the Christian life described in this book: how to study the

Bible, how to pray, the importance of involvement in the church, and how to live a godly life. By sharing some of these simple lessons, you can impact a new believer's life in a wonderful way.

Benefits of Disciple-Making

Making other disciples is extremely important, because the failure to do so will have damaging results on your own walk with Christ. Attending Bible studies and prayer meetings, reading Christian books, and listening to teaching without an outlet through which to share those truths will cause us to spiritually decay. We need to take what God gave us and use it constructively in the lives of others.

So when you take a new believer under your wing, you're not only encouraging a new child of God, you're also saving yourself from spiritual stagnation. New believers need our wisdom, knowledge, and experience, and we need the zeal, spark, and childlike faith that a young Christian possesses.

Have you ever led anyone to Jesus Christ? Have you discipled anyone? Have you taken a new believer under your wing and helped him or her along? Working with someone in this way can reignite your spiritual life as that person discovers the truths of God for the first time (and as you rediscover them).

Children are the best illustration of this process. When you're with a child, you begin to see things through a child's eyes again. As the child discovers things for the first time, you rediscover the newness of those things. It's wonderful when a child first discovers the ocean, walks on sand, picks up snow, or tastes ice cream. These are experiences that adults take for granted, but when we see a child discover them, we share in his or her excitement.

In the same way, when we see a new believer discover things from God's Word and the excitement it brings, it reignites us. Often they might ask difficult questions that will make us search the Scriptures for answers. And there are always things we have learned but forgotten. A new believer's questions can help us rediscover (or discover for the first time) many important spiritual truths.

The fact is, many mature Christians come to a point where they simply dry up. When this happens, some might begin wondering what's wrong. Some seek a solution in finding a new church or some new teaching that will revolutionize their lives. In most cases, the real problem is simply spiritual sluggishness. The person in this position should be passing along what he or she has learned to a younger believer. We have a simple choice: *evangelize or fossilize.*

Jesus said that "whoever has [or is passing it on] will be given more, and he will have abundance. Whoever does not have [or is not passing it on], even what he has will be taken from him" (Matt. 13:12 NIV). I have found this to be true: The more I give of myself, my time, my money, the more God seems to give back to me. As Proverbs 11:25 says, "The generous soul will be made rich, and he who waters will also be watered himself."

At one point the children of Israel faced the problem of spiritual stagnation. God told them through the prophet Isaiah to take their eyes off their own problems and start giving away what they had been given: "No, this is the kind of fasting I want: Free those who are wrongly imprisoned; lighten the burden of those who work for you. Let the oppressed go free, and remove the chains that bind people" (Isa. 58:6 NLT).

The reward for obedience is found a few verses later: "Then your salvation will come like the dawn, and your wounds will quickly heal. Your godliness will lead you forward, and the glory of the LORD will protect you from behind" (Isa. 58:8 NLT).

You can partake of that same promise if you open your life and disciple someone else. It can start today, right where you are, with the people God has brought into your path. Remember, *it takes one to make one.*

For the sake of those who don't yet know Jesus, don't forsake God's commission to "go and make disciples." For the sake of a young believer, don't let apathy rob you of blessing him or her as a mentor. And for the sake of maintaining your own exciting, fruitful walk with God, don't ignore these commands of Jesus. The promises and blessings are for those who apply these principles.

Indeed, the harvest is plentiful, but the laborers are few. We need more laborers, *and more disciples.* May God help you and me to be just that.

13

DISCIPLESHIP: IT'S YOUR CHOICE

And this is eternal life, that they may know
You, the only true God, and Jesus Christ
whom You have sent. (John 17:3)

It has been said that if you aim at nothing, you are bound to hit it. So
what course are you following? It is not a mystical thing: You decide
what it will be. You can choose where you end up in life.

As Moses said to the people of Israel:

> This day I call heaven and earth as witnesses against
> you that I have set before you life and death, blessings
> and curses. Now choose life, so that you and your
> children may live and that you may love the LORD
> your God, listen to his voice, and hold fast to him.
> For the LORD is your life. (Deut. 30:19–20 NIV)

The stand you make today will determine your direction tomorrow. You decide what the evening of your life will be by what you do in the morning of your life. And the good news is that even if you have made mistakes, you can still recommit yourself because you serve the God of second chances. You and I were placed on earth to know and glorify God. Everything else in life is secondary. Your career, your possessions, your family, and even your ministries, pale in comparison to knowing God.

Jesus prayed for His disciples, "Now this is eternal life: that they may know you, the only true God, and Jesus Christ, whom you have sent" (John 17:3 NIV).

God said to Jeremiah: "Let not the wise man glory in his wisdom, let not the mighty man glory in his might, nor let the rich man glory in his riches; but let him who glories glory in this, that he understands and knows Me" (Jer. 9:23–24).

This was the objective of the apostle Paul, who said, "I want to know Christ and the power of his resurrection and the fellowship of sharing in his sufferings, becoming like him in his death" (Phil. 3:10 NIV). Another translation phrases the verse this way: "that I may progressively become more deeply and intimately acquainted with Him" (AB).

Total Commitment

From his deathbed, David said these words to his son Solomon, and they still speak powerfully to us today:

> And Solomon, my son, learn to know the God of
> your ancestors intimately. Worship and serve him

with your whole heart and a willing mind. For
the LORD sees every heart and knows every plan
and thought. If you seek him, you will find him.
But if you forsake him, he will reject you forever.
(1 Chron. 28:9 NLT)

David knew what he was talking about. When he was just a boy, Samuel plucked him from obscurity to become the king of Israel. One has only to read the Psalms that David penned to discover that he loved God deeply. This young man enjoyed an extraordinary intimacy with God. That is why the Bible describes him as "the sweet psalmist of Israel" (2 Sam. 23:1) and "a man after [God's] own heart" (1 Sam. 13:14). We read about him tending sheep in the fields and singing beautiful songs of praise to God as he played his stringed instrument.

He was so adept musically that when demonic forces tormented King Saul, David played his music in praise to God, and the songs would temporarily drive those forces away. David enjoyed closeness with God and had no idea as he tended his sheep that God would one day call him to become the next king of Israel.

Of course David faced many challenges before he ascended the throne. But when his day finally came, he ruled well and with wisdom. He became a courageous warrior whom the people loved. God had blessed him.

But then David started to slip. The intimacy and closeness we read about in the early phases of his life left, and instead we see idleness. In fact, on the fateful night when he fell into sin with Bathsheba, we read, "At the time when kings go off to war … David remained in Jerusalem" (2 Sam. 11:1 NIV). Instead of leading his troops into battle, he kicked back and took a little R and R. He was looking for trouble and found it in the beautiful Bathsheba. The Bible doesn't fault Bathsheba, but clearly places the blame at the feet of this king. He was responsible for his actions.

David brought Bathsheba into his chambers, had sexual relations with her, and she became pregnant. But instead of acknowledging his sin, David had her husband Uriah brought back to make it appear as though the child were his. But Uriah didn't sleep with his wife, so David basically had Uriah put to death, covering up his sin (or so he thought), and then married Bathsheba. David thought he had pulled it off. A year passed in which he fell out of fellowship with God. Then one day, the prophet Nathan confronted David and he confessed, admitting he had sinned.

In spite of this tragic fall, the Bible tells us that David was a man after God's own heart. Why is that? Didn't he commit some serious sins? *Absolutely.* But when confronted with his sin, David admitted it. He did not minimize his sin, nor did he blame it on others. He did not label it as something else. Instead he said to the prophet Nathan, "I have sinned against the LORD" (2 Sam. 12:13).

If you want to be a man or woman after God's own heart, know this: You will sin. You will fall short. But when you realize you have sinned, don't blame others. Don't make excuses for it. Don't minimize it. Say, like David, "Against You, You only, have I sinned, and done this evil in Your sight" (Ps. 51:4). God will forgive you, as He did David, if you confess your sins to Him (1 John 1:9).

Of course, that doesn't mean you won't reap the consequences of that sin. David certainly did. Although God forgave him, he saw his own behavior repeated in the lives of his children. He learned his lessons in the school of hard knocks.

So when he realized his life was drawing to a close, David told Solomon, "Son, I am on my way out of here. You will be taking over. Here is what I have learned: You need to know God. If you understand this, everything else will fall into place. Solomon, you cannot live off my relationship with God. You must develop your own."

Note that David told Solomon to "serve [God] with wholehearted devotion and with a willing mind" (1 Chron. 28:9 NIV). In other words, our commitment to God needs to be total.

Abraham had a problem with commitment when God first called him. Like David, Abraham had a relationship with God; he was even called "the friend of God" (James 2:23 NLT). At God's command, Abraham left his pagan country and family members for a foreign land that God promised to show him. Abraham obeyed God—*sort of.* He did leave his country, but he took along some family members who dragged him down spiritually. Ultimately, Abraham broke those ties, specifically with his nephew Lot. It was after this that God came to him again and essentially renewed his commission.

Abraham threw away many years he could have spent drawing closer to God, because he only partially obeyed Him. Abraham attempted to know God with a divided heart, and God doesn't like that. He wants complete commitment.

It would be like saying to your spouse, "Honey, I love you, but I'm thinking of dating other people. Are you good with that?" *Of course not.* No one in his or her right mind would accept such an arrangement.

As for Solomon, he followed his father's advice in the beginning. When God appeared to him in a dream and said, "Ask for whatever you want me to give you" (1 Kings 3:5 NIV), Solomon replied,

> I am only a little child and do not know how to carry out my duties…. So give your servant a discerning heart to govern your people and to distinguish between right and wrong. For who is able to govern this great people of yours? (vv. 7, 9 NIV)

God told him that because he did not ask for riches, honor, or a long life, He would give Solomon the wisdom he desired. What's more, God promised to bless him with the things he hadn't asked for. Solomon got off to a great start. He had such incredible wisdom that people came from around the globe to see him. The queen of Sheba told him, "Indeed, not even half the greatness of your wisdom was told me; you have far exceeded the report I heard" (2 Chron. 9:6 NIV). He was even able to build the temple for the Lord that his father David wanted to build.

But as time passed, Solomon drifted away from knowing God. He followed in the footsteps of his father and in some ways was even worse. He went into a gross backslide. He had been there, done that, and found it unsatisfying. And at the end of it all, he concluded: "Fear God and keep his commandments, for this is the whole duty of man" (Eccl. 12:13 NIV). I believe Solomon came to recognize the wisdom of his father's admonition to know God.

It Starts with Us

The more we know God, the more we should want to make Him known to a lost world. As we look at our nation today, it is easy for us to say, "America needs revival." But let's narrow it down. Revival starts with you and me.

Carefully pore over the words of 2 Chronicles 7:14, in which God instructs His people to humble themselves and turn from their sins so He will heal their land. Commit this verse to memory. We all want to see our land healed. But notice that God directs His words to *His* people. God doesn't point His finger at Congress or the White House. He doesn't point His finger at Hollywood. He says, "*If My people* ..." We need to ask God if there is anything in our lives that isn't right with Him today, and every day.

In Jeremiah 29:11 God says that He has plans to give us "hope and a future" (NIV). The word *future* also could be translated "an expected end" or "hope in your final outcome" (AB). In other words, there will be a redemptive outcome in your life. God will tie up the loose ends. As a Christian, you are a work in progress: "He who began a good work in you will carry it on to completion until the day of Christ Jesus" (Phil. 1:6 NIV).

I am an artist. I like to draw and design and have always been interested in graphics. There are times when I'm drawing something and someone will look over my shoulder and ask, "What's it going to be?"

"Just wait," I'll say.

"I think you should do this ..." he or she might say.

"Just let me do it," I answer. "When I'm finished, I will gladly show it to you."

In the same way, each of us is a work in progress. God is doing a work in your life, and when the work is done He will show you. It's not done yet, so we have to be patient. But God sees the end from the beginning. Ecclesiastes 3:11 says, "He has made everything beautiful in its time. He has also set eternity in the hearts of men; yet they cannot fathom what God has done from beginning to end" (NIV).

We can't see the work God is doing, but He is indeed working. One day we will be free from the effects of sin and will no longer experience the limitations of the human body. Our questions will be answered, and we will live forever in the presence of God Almighty.

In the meantime, we should make it our aim to live godly lives and do whatever God tells us to do. This cannot be overemphasized. We have no right to say we know God if we don't seek to live the way He called us to live.

Talk is cheap. I believe in verbally proclaiming the gospel, but our lifestyle is vitally important. Many times our words carry no weight because we contradict them by the way that we live. As 1 John 2:3–4 reminds us, "We can be sure that we know him if we obey his commandments. If someone claims, 'I know God,' but doesn't obey God's commandments, that person is a liar and is not living in the truth" (NLT).

So as Christians, we ought to tell the truth. We should not steal. We should keep our marriage vows. And we are to be men and women of integrity because people are watching us. It's amazing how many people will say they know God but don't do what He says.

Again, Jesus said, "Let your light so shine before men, that they may see your good works and glorify your Father in heaven" (Matt. 5:16). This means that we should do good for others, including unbelievers, so they will come to know Christ. As I pointed out earlier, you are the only Bible some people will ever read.

When we truly live godly lives, it earns us the right to proclaim the gospel boldly. People can see that we're different, and as a result, they are far more open to hearing our message.

Saved Soul, Wasted Life

This discussion of discipleship may seem like Christianity 101, but my question to you is this: *Are you doing these things?* Does your life have any spiritual substance? The prophet Daniel interpreted God's words for the wicked king Belshazzar, who basically thumbed his nose at God, "You have been weighed in the balances, and found wanting" (Dan. 5:27). In other words, "Belshazzar, you have been a spiritual lightweight. You have no substance. And now your life is required of you." He wasted his life, and it was too late to change. Let that not be said of us.

If your life were to be weighed in the balances today, what would God say to you? Would He find a life of substance, a life dedicated to following Christ? Or, would He find a life that has been wasted in empty pursuits?

As a young man, Alan Redpath was a successful CPA. He had made a commitment to Christ, but wasn't really living for the Lord. One day, he was talking with a Christian friend who made a statement that altered the course of his life: "It is possible to have a saved soul and a wasted life." Redpath could not forget those words. They haunted him all that day, into the night, and throughout the next day. He couldn't let them go. He realized that God was showing him that he had a saved soul but a wasted life.

So Redpath prayed for God's will in his life, dedicating himself to God's service. God redirected his course, and instead of remaining a CPA, Redpath became a minister and served God for many years—in which he wrote a number of wonderful Christian books.

I am not suggesting that if you dedicate your life to God, He will redirect you to become a minister or a missionary, although that's possible. He might leave you right where you are but show you a new way to use your gifts for His glory. Then again, He might direct you to take a path you've never considered.

Remember this: Your life belongs to God. You're not sharing your time and talents with Him; *He is sharing His with you.* We all need to recognize and acknowledge that fact.

The attitude of a true disciple should be "Lord, I don't know how much time I have left. I may have many years. Or, I may not have as many as I hope to have. Either way, my time is in Your hands. I dedicate myself to You. You gave me the sacred trust of sharing the gospel message. I am ready to do my part."

Are you willing to make this commitment today?

My prayer is that the principles outlined in this section will help you to better understand what it means to be a true disciple of Jesus Christ—and that you might experience radical Christian living for yourself.

PART THREE

MAKING HIM KNOWN

14

FIRST-CENTURY PRINCIPLES FOR REACHING THE TWENTY-FIRST CENTURY

Does the idea of speaking to a total stranger about Christ make you nervous? Have you ever tried to tell someone about Jesus and had it go nowhere? Has someone ever asked a difficult question about your faith that you did not know how to answer?

As I will point out again later, we often overcomplicate this thing we call *evangelism*. I believe God can use you to bring others into His kingdom. Otherwise, why would God have commanded us to make disciples? We are told in Proverbs 11:30, "The fruit of the righteous is a tree of life, and he who wins souls is wise." And Daniel 12:3 says, "Those who are wise shall shine like the brightness of the firmament, and those who turn many to righteousness like the stars for ever and ever."

God wants to use you to bring others to Himself. That's a fact. Let's find out how together.

Billy Graham once said,

> The evangelistic harvest is always urgent. The des-
> tiny of men and of nations is always being decided.
> Every generation is crucial; every generation is
> strategic. But we are not responsible for the past
> generation, and we cannot bear full responsibility
> for the next one. However, we do have *our* genera-
> tion! God will hold us responsible at the Judgment
> Seat of Christ for how well we fulfilled our respon-
> sibilities and took advantage of our opportunities.[1]

I believe the world today is hungry for the message we have to offer. People are in a spiritual search mode—*especially young people.* Every day we face opportunities to share this message, opportunities we must seize. We must take hold of the moment or we may lose it forever.

I'm well aware that we live in a postmodern world where moral relativism is the rule of the day. Some people may feel as though the time to present absolute truth has passed. We can only ask ques-tions, not offer answers, they might say. But, to borrow a phrase from the British, that's *rubbish.* Regardless of the trends of contemporary culture, truth is still truth. In spite of our dramatic advances in tech-nology, the essential needs of humanity remain the same. And so does the answer to its problems.

God calls us to bring the gospel to our generation, but many of us fail in this regard. Perhaps this is because many Christians are out of touch with our culture. Some of us seem to have forgotten that we live in the twenty-first century.

This reminds me of the woman who accompanied her husband to his doctor's appointment. Afterward, the doctor called her into his office and said, "Your husband is suffering from a very severe disease, combined with horrible stress. If you don't do the following, your husband will surely die.

"Each morning, fix him a healthy breakfast. Be pleasant, and make sure he is in a good mood. For lunch, make him a nutritious meal. For dinner, prepare an especially nice meal for him. Don't burden him with chores, as he probably will have had a hard day. Don't discuss your problems with him; it only will make his stress worse. And, most importantly, smother your husband with affection and kiss him constantly. Make every effort to satisfy his every whim.

"If you can do this for the next ten to twelve months, then I think your husband will regain his health completely."

On the way home, the husband asked his wife, "So, what did the doctor say?"

"You're going to die," she replied.

Like this woman, some Christians would rather disregard a lost soul than change how they live. We live in a sin-sick world, and we need to do everything we can to reach people. As God told the prophet Isaiah, "So is my word that goes out from my mouth: It will not return to me empty, but will accomplish what I desire and achieve the purpose for which I sent it" (Isa. 55:11 NIV).

Paul's Playbook

I believe that the principles used in the first century for proclaiming the gospel still work today. In Acts 17 we observe Paul, a master communicator, bringing his message to Athens. At that time, Athens was the cultural and intellectual center of the world, carrying the legacy of the great philosophers Socrates, Plato, Aristotle, and others who established patterns of thought that have affected human learning for centuries. Almost all philosophies follow, to some degree, the teachings of these men.

While Paul was in Athens, he did what any tourist would do. He went sightseeing. There were magnificent architectural edifices, statues, and images erected to many deities. But he was grieved to see the absolute absence of the living God. Instead, he found every imaginable substitute.

Have you ever felt that way looking at our own confused society? Do you ever find yourself channel surfing, and as you look at all of the things that are being offered to our culture today, you get angry? We have a choice: We can wring our hands in exasperation and complain about the state of affairs in our world. Or, we can do something about it: *Take the gospel to the world.*

Paul could have cursed the darkness, but instead he turned on the light. And that brings us to our first principle of effective evangelism.

Principle 1: Effective Evangelism Begins with a Burden

Paul's message to the Athenians began when God stirred his spirit. He was grieved to see the absence of the living God and every conceivable substitute in His place. So Paul took action:

> While Paul was waiting for them in Athens, he
> was greatly distressed to see that the city was full
> of idols. So he reasoned in the synagogue with the
> Jews and the God-fearing Greeks, as well as in the

> marketplace day by day with those who happened
> to be there. (Acts 17:16–17 NIV)

The phrase *greatly distressed* in verse 16 could be literally translated "exasperated" or "irritated and roused to anger." In other words, Paul was hot and mad.

Moved to Action

One of the reasons we don't always reach our culture effectively is because we are woefully out of touch, living in our own Christian subculture. And honestly, many of us don't care about people who don't know the Lord. This is hard for some of us to admit. If we were brutally honest, we would have to say that we don't have that burden. However, Paul felt so burdened that he declared, "Woe is me if I do not preach the gospel!" (1 Cor. 9:16). We simply have to care, or nothing will happen in the way of effective evangelism.

Does your heart ache for lost people?

C. H. Spurgeon knew the need for such a burden when he said, "The Holy Spirit will move them by first moving you. If you can rest without their being saved, they will rest too. But if you are filled with an agony for them, and if you cannot bear that they should be lost, you will soon find that they are uneasy too."[2]

Principle 2: Effective Evangelists Need to Know Their Audience

We need to know the people to whom we speak. Paul went right to these people and brought the gospel to them. It's important for us to have contact with—to be among—people who need the gospel. Jesus certainly modeled this. Time and time again, we see Him breaking free from the multitudes to bring the message to one individual. From the midst of a crowd, He called Zacchaeus out of a tree. In the blazing noonday sun, He engaged a Samaritan woman in conversation. And He managed a late-night meeting with the religious man, Nicodemus. Jesus always had time for people, and we should too, be it day or night.

Build a Bridge

One of the best ways to share the gospel is simply to listen and ask questions. I have discovered that everyone's favorite subject is himself or herself. We can easily turn a monologue into a dialogue by saying, "Tell me about yourself," or asking, "What do you think about this or that?" As you do so, you learn about and better understand that person. And because you've taken the time to listen to what the other person has to say, it's more likely he or she will listen to you.

We see Paul taking the time to familiarize himself with the Athenians and what they believed. He examined their idols. He read their poems. He understood their culture. And he wanted to build a bridge to them:

> So he reasoned in the synagogue with the Jews and
> the God-fearing Greeks, as well as in the marketplace
> day by day with those who happened to be there.
> A group of Epicurean and Stoic philosophers began
> to dispute with him. Some of them asked, "What is
> this babbler trying to say?" Others remarked, "He
> seems to be advocating foreign gods." They said this

because Paul was preaching the good news about Jesus and the resurrection. (Acts 17:17–18 NIV).

The Epicureans and the Stoics

There were two primary groups that Paul addressed in Athens: the Epicureans and the Stoics, representing the two dominant schools of thought at that time.

According to the founder of the Epicureans, Epicurus, the chief goal of life was to attain the maximum amount of pleasure and the minimum amount of pain. The Epicureans believed the world came about by chance, a random concourse of atoms, and that there would be no afterlife or future judgment. Their basic belief was that this life is all there is. You only go around once, so if it feels good, *do it*. If it doesn't feel good, don't do it. Avoid what hurts or causes pain. You could say they were the party animals of the first century.

The Epicurean mentality is still with us today; we see this way of thinking everywhere in our culture. The Bible even points out that this mind-set will be prevalent in the last days: "But know this, that in the last days perilous times will come: For men will be lovers of themselves ... without self-control ... headstrong, *haughty, lovers of pleasure rather than lovers of God*" (2 Tim. 3:1–4). The Bible also warns against embracing this philosophy, saying those who live for pleasure are dead already (1 Tim. 5:6).

In contrast to the Epicureans, the Stoics were more disciplined, shunning the pursuit of pleasure. Founded by a man name Zeno, the Stoic philosophy taught *self-mastery*. The Stoics' goal in life was to reach a place of indifference to either pleasure or pain. Zeno taught that life is filled with good and bad. Because you cannot avoid the bad, you must try to grin and bear it. The Stoics believed that God was in everything material: in the trees, plants, animals, mountains, and fields. The Stoics' descendants are among us today as well. These are people who have no sense of God or His will for their lives. They do the best they can, and if bad comes, they try to stay strong and endure.

Yet both of these philosophies are wrong because they both reject God. After all, if you don't know God, then you must put something in His place.

Principle 3: Effective Evangelism Must Be Culturally Relevant

Paul could have blasted his listeners with both barrels. But amazingly, he sought to build a bridge to them and quoted one of their own poets: "For in Him we live and move and have our being, as also some of your own poets have said, 'For we are also His offspring'" (Acts 17:28).

It is so important that our listeners know that we live in the same world they do. We don't necessarily want to build our message on current issues, but to completely ignore the culture we live in is to miss an opportunity. Far too often, those of us called to communicate are out of touch with others. The Bible speaks of the leaders of the tribe of Issachar, "who had understanding of the times, to know what Israel ought to do" (1 Chron. 12:32).

The Downside of a Christian Subculture

Some Christians can immerse themselves in the Christian subculture with a language that no one else can understand: "Are you washed in the blood, sanctified, and a part of the body?" and "Just make sure you are not living in the flesh!" Meanwhile, the person listening is thinking, *Let's see, I need to be part of the body, but not live in the flesh?*

I'm not suggesting that we stop using biblical terms; we just need to better define them. Far too often, we answer questions no one is asking and fail to answer the ones they are.

Jesus made an interesting statement on this subject: "For the people of this world are more shrewd in dealing with their own kind than are the people of the light" (Luke 16:8 NIV). The "people of this world" are far shrewder in the way they present their message and advertise their wares. Meanwhile, the Christian community often puts out mediocre presentations. The problem is that the devil never goes on vacation. He never goes to sleep. He is ever vigilant to pull more and more people into his web of destruction.

A number of years ago I was invited to address the members of the National Religious Broadcasters at their annual convention. I asked why we settle for mediocrity and low standards in the Christian media. We no longer live in the 1950s; it's the twenty-first century. Why can't our graphics be cutting-edge? Why can't our music be fresh and original—rather than rehashed copies? Why can't our TV and radio productions be attuned to the culture? Why can't our movies be better crafted and created with artistic integrity? I believe these things can happen. At the time of this writing, Christian music and movies with a faith message have dramatically advanced.

I am not arguing for sensationalism, although I would prefer that to stagnation. I will not compromise our message one bit. But Jesus did say that the sons of this world are shrewder in their generation than we are. So I say, let's beat them at their own game. Be culturally relevant and speak their language, but deliver the message they need to hear.

The problem often lies in the out-of-touch, even bizarre way we present our message. I would venture to say there are some Christians today who are not persecuted for righteousness' sake—they are persecuted for being just plain weird!

Keep It Interesting

Paul's message aroused the interest of his listeners. And the first thing he did was to build a bridge to his audience:

> Paul then stood up in the meeting of the Areopagus and said: "Men of Athens! I see that in every way you are very religious. For as I walked around and looked carefully at your objects of worship, I even found an altar with this inscription: TO AN UNKNOWN GOD. Now what you worship as something unknown I am going to proclaim to you." (Acts 17:22–23 NIV)

What a diplomatic way for Paul to begin his message! He could have said, "You're a bunch of pagans, and you're going to burn in hell!" Technically, that would have been true. But the objective of effective communication is to build a bridge, not burn one. So Paul found something in common with these people. Along the same lines, he said,

> Even though I am a free man with no master, I have become a slave to all people to bring many to

Christ.… Yes, I try to find common ground with everyone, doing everything I can to save some. I do everything to spread the Good News and share in its blessings. (1 Cor. 9:19, 22–23 NLT)

Far too often, unbelievers know Christians only for what we stand against, not what we stand for. They know we're against abortion, sexual immorality, and same-sex marriage. But do they know we stand for Jesus? Religious leaders criticized Jesus for eating and drinking with sinners. But He did this to reach them rather than repel them.

The classic example is Jesus' encounter with the Samaritan woman, whom I mentioned earlier. He could have said, "You are an immoral woman, and you're going to hell!" But instead, He talked with her. The Bible says that it is the goodness of God that leads us to repentance (Rom. 2:4). Jesus appealed to the emptiness inside her that drove her to immorality, and He gained a real convert that day.

I heard a story about a minister who was asked to say a few words at a luncheon. He had been instructed to speak for about five minutes, but soon he reached ten minutes and then fifteen minutes. The moderator cleared his throat, hoping the good reverend would notice it was time to stop. The preacher continued to speak.

So the moderator actually pounded his gavel to get his attention. But on the minister droned. Twenty minutes passed, and people grew upset. A few walked out. Finally, the moderator continuously pounded his gavel, hoping the preacher would cease. Still, the minister did not stop speaking. In frustration, the moderator threw his gavel at the preacher, narrowly missing him. The gavel hit an elderly man who had fallen asleep in the front row. The man woke up, heard the preacher, and mumbled to the moderator, "Hit me again! I can still hear him!"

There is no excuse for communicating the gospel poorly. Paul said, "For I am not ashamed of the gospel of Christ, for it is the power of God to salvation" (Rom. 1:16). There is explosive power in the gospel. We don't need to add to it or take away from it. We don't need to complicate it or gloss it over. We just need to proclaim it and allow God to work.

Principle 4: Effective Evangelism Must Be Biblical

Paul's message was biblical. He opened with a cultural connection and then took his listeners to the Word of God. This is important because, as I wrote earlier, God's Word will never return void (Isa. 55:11). In other words, the gospel will always bear fruit. I have heard so many evangelists begin with a humorous illustration or a tear-jerking story and build their entire message on that illustration. They might read a biblical text and then return to their stories and jokes. I believe this is a grave error. Never build a message on an illustration. Always build it on the Word of God. God did not say that clever illustrations would not return void; He said that His Word would not return void.

The great preacher C. H. Spurgeon said, "A sermon without illustrations is like a room without windows."[3] We don't want to build a house of glass or a house without any windows. I have seen that glazed look on people's faces as I am explaining a term like *justification,* only to see them spring back after a simple illustration.

Certainly Jesus modeled this for us in His use of parables, which are earthly stories with a heavenly meaning—illustrations, in other words. Matthew 13:34 tells us, "Jesus always used stories and illustrations like these when speaking to the crowds. In fact, he never spoke to them without using such parables" (NLT).

The Power Source

Illustrations certainly have their place, but the power is in God's Word. Paul reminded Timothy of the power of Scripture:

> From infancy you have known the holy Scriptures, which are able to make you wise for salvation through faith in Christ Jesus. All Scripture is God-breathed and is useful for teaching, rebuking, correcting and training in righteousness, so that the man of God may be thoroughly equipped for every good work. (2 Tim. 3:15–17 NIV)

The word *useful* in verse 16 focuses on the fact that Scripture is sufficient. Everything we need to know about God is found in the Bible. We don't need some "new" revelation. The objective is not to make the Bible relevant, because it *is* relevant. However, if we do not believe, as Paul stated, that "all Scripture is given by inspiration of God," then we will have problems from the very beginning.

Principle 5: Effective Evangelism Focuses on Jesus

An effective evangelistic message will always go to the cross. Paul concluded his message in Athens by saying, "For he has set a day when he will judge the world with justice by the man he has appointed. He has given proof of this to all men by raising him from the dead" (Acts 17:31 NIV). I am amazed when I hear entire evangelistic messages that make only a passing reference to the cross.

I once asked Billy Graham, "After all these years of preaching, if you knew as a younger preacher what you know now, what would you emphasize more?" Without a missing a beat, he replied, "I would preach more on the cross of Christ and on the blood. That is where the power is." How important that is! And when we fail to do this, we water down the message of the gospel.

Paul gave this same warning, pointing out that God had called him "to preach the gospel, not with wisdom of words, lest the cross of Christ should be made of no effect. For the message of the cross is foolishness to those who are perishing, but to us who are being saved it is the power of God" (1 Cor. 1:17–18). The phrase *of no effect* could be literally translated "deprived of its power."

Paul also said that he "resolved to know nothing … except Jesus Christ and him crucified" (1 Cor. 2:2 NIV). Paul recognized the distinct power in the simple message of the life, death, and resurrection of Jesus Christ.

Principle 6: Effective Evangelism Presents the Whole Gospel

Paul also used a word that we rarely hear these days: *repent.* He told his audience in Athens,

> Truly, these times of ignorance God overlooked,
> but now commands all men everywhere to repent,
> because He has appointed a day on which He will

judge the world in righteousness by the Man whom
He has ordained. He has given assurance of this to
all by raising Him from the dead. (Acts 17:30–31)

This was a command from God Himself. Paul didn't say, "I'd suggest you repent," or "I'd advise you to repent," or even "I hope you
repent." Paul said that God "commands all men everywhere to repent."
Then he went on to give three reasons why they should repent:

1. *There is a day of judgment coming (Acts 17:30).*
God has appointed a day on which He will judge
the world.
2. *There is an unchallengeable Judge (v. 31).* The one
who will do the evaluating will be God.
3. *There is an irrefutable fact (v. 31).* God has made
this irrefutably evident by raising this Man (Jesus)
from the dead.

The Entire Gospel

Rarely do we hear about judgment in our day and age. Yet if
we fail to talk about it, we fail to declare the whole counsel of God.
I'm not suggesting that we preach only "hellfire and brimstone,"
but we do want to help people fully appreciate the good news of
Jesus Christ. To do that, they must first understand the bad news of
their situation. If we don't tell people they need to repent, we haven't
shared the entire gospel.

There are a lot of people who feel remorse for their sin, but
they never truly repent. Remorse is feeling sorry, while repentance

is being sorry enough to stop. "Godly sorrow brings repentance that leads to salvation and leaves no regret, but worldly sorrow brings death" (2 Cor. 7:10 NIV).

There is such a thing as phony repentance. Phony repentance is like crying when you chop an onion: The eye sheds tears because it is irritated—not because the heart is broken. Repentance means a change of mind and a confession of wrongdoing. It means to turn around, to change one's direction, and to change *both* the mind and the will. Repentance does not denote just any change, but is always a change from wrong to right, away from sin toward righteousness.

When Paul stood before the Roman governor Agrippa, he spoke of how on the road to Damascus Jesus met him and told him,

> I will rescue you from your own people and from the Gentiles. I am sending you to them *to open their eyes and turn them from darkness to light,* and *from the power of Satan to God,* so that they may *receive forgiveness of sins* and a place among those who are sanctified by faith in me. (Acts 26:17–18 NIV)

Paul laid out for Agrippa (and for us today) the process of salvation, which clearly includes repentance:

1. We must have our spiritual eyes opened.
2. We must turn from darkness to light and from the power of Satan to God.

3. We will receive, as a result, the forgiveness of sins and an inheritance.

Paul told his listeners there was a coming judgment. And he told them they needed to repent. Yet this is absent from much discourse today. Our job is not to make people feel good. *Our job is to tell them the truth.*

Principle 7: Effective Evangelism Leaves the Results to God

God will hold us responsible for proclaiming the truth and being faithful. But after that, the rest is up to Him. Even the great apostle Paul had days when the response was minimal. I take comfort from the fact that one of the greatest communicators of all time didn't always have the most successful meetings imaginable:

> And when they heard of the resurrection of the dead, some mocked, while others said, "We will hear you again on this matter." So Paul departed from among them. However, some men joined him and believed, among them Dionysius the Areopagite, a woman named Damaris, and others with them. (Acts 17:32–34)

Reactions to the Gospel

The word *mocked* in verse 32 could be translated "some of them sneered and burst out laughing." Paul had just shared the gospel, and they laughed in his face. These elitists, who thought they were so brilliant, dismissed the preaching of the gospel by one of the greatest preachers in the history of the church.

This is a reminder that no matter how effectively you communicate, some people will react with scorn. And that will hurt. But it happened to Paul; it will happen to you. That's why you need to pray that God will open their eyes and help them see the reality of what you are saying.

While some mocked, others procrastinated. They succumbed to the curse of intellectual, academic detachment. They used the delay tactic: "We will hear you again on this matter" (v. 32). Many intellectuals today use the same tactic: "You know, those are interesting points you've brought up. I will think about this."

Even though some mocked and some delayed, some believed: "However, some men joined him and believed, among them Dionysius the Areopagite, a woman named Damaris, and others with them" (v. 34). Dionysius the Areopagite was one of the judges, an intellectual and a ruler of the city.

D. L. Moody once said, "I would a great deal rather see a hundred men thoroughly converted, truly born of God, than to see a thousand professed conversions where the Spirit of God has not convicted of sin."[4] I would rather see a few people who really understand the gospel respond to its message than a multitude who don't have a clue.

Conversion is the work of God and God alone. Yes, He uses us, but we must completely depend on Him for the results. Many of our attempts at sharing the gospel fail because we do so in our own strength. We are like the disciples who fished all night and caught nothing, only to see everything change when Jesus came on board.

It's actually a great relief to know that my responsibility is to lovingly, accurately, and clearly proclaim the gospel. The actual work of conversion is God's job. Jesus said, "No one can come to Me unless the Father who sent Me draws him; and I will raise him up at the last day" (John 6:44).

We need to remember that it's all in the hands of God. At the same time, we are foolish to congratulate ourselves for great successes. We are also fools to condemn ourselves for times when our message doesn't resonate. *It is the gospel.* The results are always up to Him. All that God holds us responsible for is faithfulness in proclamation, not how many people were in attendance or how many responded. That's not our job.

People don't convert people—*the Holy Spirit converts people.*

Our job is to proclaim the gospel faithfully, lovingly, accurately, and understandably, and then let the Lord do His work with His message in His way.

———

The Seven Principles of Effective Evangelism

Principle 1: Effective Evangelism Begins with a Burden.

Principle 2: Effective Evangelists Need to Know Their Audience.

Principle 3: Effective Evangelism Must Be Culturally Relevant.

Principle 4: Effective Evangelism Must Be Biblical.

Principle 5: Effective Evangelism Focuses on Jesus.

Principle 6: Effective Evangelism Presents the Whole Gospel.

Principle 7: Effective Evangelism Leaves the Results to God.

———————

15

THE THREE Ws OF EVANGELISM

The first time I attempted to share my faith, I was seventeen years old and had been a Christian for two weeks. I heard that I was supposed to go out and tell others about Jesus. So I thought, *Well, I've been a believer now for two entire weeks. I know quite a bit.* It seemed like I knew a lot at the time—a lot more than I used to know, at least. I also knew that I wanted to share what God had done for me because my life had changed so dramatically.

So I went out on the beach, armed with my Bible and a copy of a little booklet from Campus Crusade for Christ called *The Four Spiritual Laws.*[1] This material was so new to me that I hadn't even memorized its contents yet. As I walked along looking for someone who wouldn't give me too hard of a time, I saw a woman who looked about the same age as my mother. I thought she'd be pretty friendly.

As I walked up to her, I was so nervous. My mouth was dry. With voice shaking, I said, "Hi. How are you today?"

She looked at me. "Fine, young man. How are you?"

"Oh, I am really good. Yeah. You know, I ... I just ... uh, you know, I wanted to read something to you. Could I do that?"

"Sure."

So I sat down and started to read that little booklet verbatim. As I said, I hadn't even memorized it yet. "*The Four Spiritual Laws....* Law one: God loves you and has a wonderful plan for your life...." And I kept reading, page after page.

Meanwhile, I was thinking to myself, *What on earth am I doing? There's no way she'll become a Christian. This is a complete waste of time.* But then I thought, *I'm already committed. I have to finish.* So I just kept reading until I reached the last sentence: "Is there any good reason why you should not accept Jesus Christ right now?"

Realizing I had just read a question, I looked up at her.

She said no.

"Okay ... no." I looked back down at the booklet. Then it dawned on me. I looked up at her again. "Does that mean yes—you want to accept Christ right now?"

She said, "Yes, I do."

"Well, let's just bow our heads for a word of prayer," I said in the most reverent tone I could muster. (I had heard the pastor at church do that.)

As she closed her eyes, I frantically searched the booklet for what to do next. I had planned for failure and not success. Eventually I found a prayer, which she repeated after me. Meanwhile, I was thinking, *This isn't going to work. This isn't real. This can't be happening.*

But it was.

When I finished praying, she opened her eyes and said, "Something just happened to me."

Something had just happened to me, too. I got a taste of what it was like to be used by God! I was so young in the faith I didn't know that in most circles, the approach I had just used would have fallen far short as a model for personal evangelism. Though I had very little information, I had a burden for non-Christians. A lot of it had to do with what God had done for me, because as Jesus said, "For everyone to whom much is given, from him much will be required; and to whom much has been committed, of him they will ask the more" (Luke 12:48). I had been as lost as a person could be, but God graciously called me to Himself and forgave me.

There is something to be said for the excitement of youth. It's probably why kids are so tech-savvy and can fix their parents' computers. Adults are afraid to try. But kids jump right in and start pushing buttons.

I'm not suggesting that we should not prepare ourselves to share the gospel. But I am suggesting that sometimes we overcomplicate this thing we call evangelism.

In this chapter, I want to look at the three Ws of evangelism— the *who, where,* and the *why.* Let's start with *who.*

The First *W:* Who?

Who is called to go into all the world and preach the gospel? Answer: *We are.* Let's reread the passage known as the Great Commission:

> Therefore go and make disciples of all nations, baptizing them in the name of the Father and of the Son and of the Holy Spirit, and teaching them to obey everything I have commanded you. And

surely I am with you always, to the very end of the
age. (Matt. 28:19–20 NIV)

In the original language, these words are addressed to everyone—
not only pastors, evangelists, and missionaries—but everyone, from
business owners to homemakers to students. *No one is exempt.*

Also, in the original language, these words are *a command.* Jesus
was not saying, "If you can find time in your busy schedules, as a
personal favor to Me, would you mind at least making an attempt
to go into all the world and preach the gospel?" He said, "As your
Commander in Chief and as your Lord, as your Master who pur-
chased you with His own blood, I am commanding you—I am
ordering you—to go into the world and preach the gospel."

The Bible says that Christ redeemed us. The word *redeem* is an
interesting word that literally means "to be bought out of a slave
market." Imagine being a slave in shackles, about to be sold to the
highest bidder, when Jesus arrives and purchases you. Then He tells
you that you're free. Wouldn't you want to serve Him for the rest of
your life? As Paul reminds us, "Do you not know that your body is
the temple of the Holy Spirit who is in you, whom you have from
God, and you are not your own? For you were bought at a price;
therefore glorify God in your body and in your spirit, which are
God's" (1 Cor. 6:19–20).

As we recognize all that God has done for us, it should be our
delight, our joy, and our privilege to obey His command to go into
all the world and preach the gospel. These words are given to every
disciple of Jesus. We should all be saying, "Lord, what is it that You
want me to do? I want to fulfill Your command."

In other words, the Great Commission of Matthew 28:19–20 is not the Great Suggestion. Since I am His disciple, I am commanded to go and make disciples of others. If I'm not making disciples of others, then I'm not really being the disciple He commanded me to be. But for many of us, it is the Great Omission instead of the Great Commission. We are simply not fulfilling it. This is a sin, as James 4:17 tells us: "Anyone, then, who knows the good he ought to do and doesn't do it, sins" (NIV).

While it may be true that not every believer has been gifted as an evangelist, it is also true that Jesus called every believer to evangelism. The idea of evangelism seems daunting, overwhelming. *How can we do it?* As has been said, the way to eat an elephant is one bite at a time. And the way to fulfill the Great Commission is one person at a time. This brings us to the second *W* of evangelism.

The Second *W:* Where?

Where are we called to preach the gospel? Answer: *Everywhere.* In Mark, we are given a variation of the Great Commission: "He said to them, 'Go into all the world and preach the good news to all creation'" (Mark 16:15 NIV).

Former Speaker of the House Tip O'Neill once said, "All politics is local,"[2] and I believe the same could be said of evangelism. Go into all *your* world and preach the gospel—into your family, your workplace, your campus, your sphere of influence.

Jesus began the Great Commission with "Therefore go and make disciples of all nations" (Matt. 28:19 NIV). Why is the word *therefore* in this sentence? We find the answer in the previous verse: "Then Jesus came to them and said, 'All authority in heaven and on earth has been given to me'" (v. 18 NIV). If the authority is in Him, and He lives inside His followers, then His power and resources are at our disposal to accomplish this task.

Now let's look at the third *W* of evangelism.

The Third *W:* Why?

Why are we to share the gospel? Answer: *God has chosen to reach people through people.* Why doesn't God simply poke His face out of the heavens and say, "Believe in Me"? Why does He want to use flawed people like us? I don't know the answer to those questions, but I know that this is His plan. As Romans 10:14–15 reminds us,

> How then shall they call on Him in whom they have not believed? And how shall they believe in Him of whom they have not heard? And how shall they hear without a preacher? And how shall they preach unless they are sent? As it is written: *"How beautiful are the feet of those who preach the gospel of peace, who bring glad tidings of good things!"*

The primary way God decided to reach people is through people like you and me.

What About "Lifestyle" Evangelism?

The primary way we must share the gospel is through our words. That is not to say that you should not live it first, for indeed you should. But the Bible does not advocate what some call "lifestyle evangelism," essentially meaning that we just live good Christian lives and wait for someone to ask us about it. It's a wonderful compliment when that happens, but at the same time, we need to initiate verbalizing our faith.

Let's look again at Acts 8 and the story of the wealthy dignitary from Ethiopia searching for God. Instead of the vibrant faith of David and Solomon, this man found a cold, dead, ritualistic faith that offered him little. Somehow he obtained a scroll containing Isaiah 53. As he read the words "he was led as a lamb to the slaughter, and as a sheep before its shearers is silent" (Isa. 53:7), Philip approached him and asked if he understood what he was reading. The dignitary replied, "How can I, unless someone guides me?" (Acts 8:31). That is what people need and what many want: *someone like you to show them the way.*

You might find this surprising, but it's not always easy for me to share the gospel. When I'm behind the pulpit, it's relatively easy. But when I share with someone one-on-one, that's a different thing altogether. There's one thing Christians and non-Christians have in common: *They are both uptight about evangelism.* Non-Christians feel uptight about being evangelized, and Christians feel uptight about evangelizing.

When I was a teenager hanging around in Newport Beach, I would see the Christians walking around, handing out their little gospel tracts. I would lean against a wall, acting like I didn't care, when all the while my heart cried, *Would you come and talk to me right now?* The problem was that they bought into my tough-guy facade. They would walk up and thrust their tracts in my direction, saying, "Here … read this." I would shove the tract into my pocket, acting as though I didn't care. But I never threw one away.

At home I had a drawer where I kept all religious literature given to me by any person of any kind of faith whatsoever. Every now and then, I would pull out this drawer, dump it on my bed, and try to figure out what it all meant. I needed someone to show me the way. I was waiting for that. I think that's what most people are searching for: *someone like you.* And again, the primary way we are to share this message is verbally. As 1 Corinthians 1:21 tells us, "For since in the wisdom of God the world through its wisdom did not know him, God was pleased through the foolishness of what was preached to save those who believe" (NIV).

Yet many of us give up so easily. We might invite our unbelieving friends to church or a Christian event, and when they say no, we'll never approach the subject again. *Do we really believe what we claim we believe?* Do we believe that there really is a heaven and hell, and that the wages of sin really is death? If so, how can we be so casual about telling others?

This comes back to the *why* of evangelism. Why should we tell others about Jesus? Because the Lord told us to, and because our words are the primary way this is done. But that brings me back to an issue I raised earlier. *We should also share the gospel because we care.* Do you have a burden, a heart for people who do not know the Lord? Sometimes we see them as enemies rather than people trapped by sin. Yet the Bible describes it in a different way:

> A servant of the Lord must not quarrel but must be
> kind to everyone, be able to teach, and be patient
> with difficult people. Gently instruct those who
> oppose the truth. Perhaps God will change those

> people's hearts, and they will learn the truth. Then
> they will come to their senses and escape from the
> devil's trap. For they have been held captive by him
> to do whatever he wants. (2 Tim. 2:24–26 NLT)

People can tell whether you really care about them. Many years ago in England, a criminal named Charles Peace was arrested and condemned to death. He had been a burglar, a forger, and was guilty of a double murder. As he was on his way to the gallows, the chaplain who walked by his side mechanically went through his often-repeated speech about the power of Jesus Christ to save from sin. Suddenly Charles Peace stopped, looked at the minister, and said, "If I believed what you say, I would crawl across England on broken glass on my hands and knees to tell men it was true!"[3]

If we really believe what we claim to believe, why aren't we doing more to get the message out? *Jesus cares about people, and so should we.*

The Need for Evangelism

Having looked at the *who, where,* and *why* of evangelism, let's look at what Jesus tells us about the need for evangelism. In the following passage, we come to a crucial time in Jesus' life and ministry. A new phase had begun. His Galilean ministry was over, and the long, slow journey to Jerusalem had begun as "He steadfastly set His face to go to Jerusalem" (Luke 9:51). To prepare the way, He selected seventy-two new disciples to go before Him.

> After this the Lord appointed seventy-two others and
> sent them two by two ahead of him to every town

and place where he was about to go. He told them,
"The harvest is plentiful, but the workers are few.
Ask the Lord of the harvest, therefore, to send out
workers into his harvest field." (Luke 10:1–2 NIV)

From this passage, we can draw direct parallels to our own lives and times. Like these seventy-two who prepared the way for Jesus' arrival, we prepare the way for His return. These are critical times for sharing the gospel. Jesus expressed a similar idea in John 4:35: "I tell you, open your eyes and look at the fields! *They are ripe for harvest*" (NIV).

In these words we see the heart of God toward this world. Clearly, from this passage and others, Jesus cared deeply about people. Matthew's gospel tells us He was "moved with compassion" for the multitudes (Matt. 9:36; 14:14). Everywhere Jesus went people mobbed Him, always wanting something from Him. But Jesus saw through to their deepest needs, where they hurt the most. He saw behind their masks and defense mechanisms, He heard the cry of their hearts. He saw them as sheep without a shepherd, going astray—*and He had compassion.*

People put up a front and pretend to be happy when they're not. But deep down inside, we all share the same hurts, desires, and needs. Today, just as in Jesus' day, the fields are "ripe for harvest."

Billy Graham: Four Universal Truths

When Billy Graham spoke to itinerant evangelists in Amsterdam in 1983, he told them he had found certain common elements in every culture he encountered. He said, "When I go out and proclaim the Gospel … whether it's on a street corner in Nairobi; or a meeting in

Seoul, Korea … I know there are certain things that are true in the hearts and minds of all people."[4]

First, Graham said there is an essential emptiness in every life without Christ. All humanity keeps crying for something, but they do not know what it is. Pascal said it well when he stated, "There is a God-shaped vacuum in every life that only God can fill" (modern paraphrase).[5] Romans 8:20–21 says, "For the creation was subjected to frustration, not by its own choice, but by the will of the one who subjected it, in hope that the creation itself will be liberated from its bondage to decay and brought into the glorious freedom of the children of God" (NIV).

Second, Graham said we can assume our listeners are lonely. You can be in a crowd of people, even at a party, and suddenly have a wave of loneliness sweep over you, a sense that you are all alone in this world.

Third, Graham said all people have a sense of guilt. The reason people feel guilt is because God gave them a conscience. As Romans 2:15 says, "They demonstrate that God's law is written in their hearts, for their own conscience and thoughts either accuse them or tell them they are doing right" (NLT).

Fourth, he said people have a universal fear of death. Death frightens us because we fear the unknown. The Bible speaks of "those who through fear of death were all their lifetime subject to bondage" (Heb. 2:15). Again, two unchallengeable truths are that we all want to be happy, and we're all going to die.

So we need to look past the facade and see the empty, lonely, guilty person in front of us. Jesus said, "For the Son of Man has come to seek and to save that which was lost" (Luke 19:10). The word *lost* speaks of something that has value but is simply broken. Some of us have a hard time separating the sin from the sinner, forgetting that we are to love the sinner and hate the sin. But if we want to reflect the heart of God, then we have to care about people—specifically unbelieving people. They're not the enemy; they're sheep without a shepherd. And lest we forget, it wasn't all that long ago that you and I were among them.

Thankfully, the Lord brought us to our senses. And without knowing your personal story, I would venture to say that He did that through human instruments: people who sowed seeds in your life over a number of years. And most likely, it was a single person who articulated the gospel for you when suddenly the lights went on. Thank God for that person!

But here is the question: *Will you be a person like that for someone else?*

What God Values

A person's soul is of the greatest value to God, and should be to us as well. When Jesus said, "The harvest truly is great, but the laborers are few" (Luke 10:2), He conveyed that the people with whom we share the gospel have great value in God's sight. Jesus did not compare them to blades of grass, sands of the sea, or dust in the wind, but to sheaves of wheat. Just as wheat is valuable to a farmer, the souls of humanity are valuable to God. Of all God's creation, people are the most precious to Him. And He values us so much that He sent His very Son to spill His blood for us. God has said, "Behold, all souls are Mine; the soul of the father as well as the soul of the son is Mine; the soul who sins shall die" (Ezek. 18:4).

My wife and I were in a restaurant one day when our server told us that I had dedicated her as a young girl. I asked her how she was doing spiritually, and she said she was doing well. But when she returned about five minutes later, she told us that some years before, she had an unplanned pregnancy and made an appointment to have an abortion. But the day before the appointment, she heard one of my messages and changed her mind. She told us that her daughter was now six years old. How I thank God for the decision that young mother made! It's the power of the Word of God.

That's why I preach the gospel and teach the Bible. That is why I do what I do and why you must do what you can do as a disciple of Jesus Christ. That little six-year-old girl now has a shot at growing up, knowing the Lord, marrying, and having children. And perhaps her children will have children, each one a precious soul to God.

Souls are valuable to God, and His heart yearns for their return to Him. From Genesis to Revelation, we see God calling humanity to Himself.

Looking for Laborers

I came to faith at an open meeting, through what some might call mass or large-scale evangelism. No one personally invited me to that meeting, no one had ever taken me aside and shared the gospel with me one-on-one. Even so, I heard the gospel proclaimed at that meeting, and I responded.

My experience isn't unique.

At an Anaheim Harvest Crusade a few years ago, one person who made a decision for Christ told an event volunteer that he was on his way to rob a liquor store when he noticed the stadium lights were on.

He decided to find out what was going on, came into the stadium, heard the gospel, walked forward at the invitation, and committed his life to Jesus Christ!

Do I really believe that all the people who respond to the invitation are truly coming to the Lord? *No, I don't.* But I also believe there are thousands who do make genuine commitments to Christ. Not only that, but many of them have gone into full-time ministry as pastors and missionaries. I attended a pastors' conference once where I talked to four pastors who each told me, independent of one another, they had come to Christ at a Harvest Crusade and were now planting their own churches and reaching people.

My "job" is to proclaim the gospel to people in a biblical, compassionate, and clear way. God's job is to convert them. And I want to use every means at my disposal to do my part well.

I remember reading about someone who criticized the great evangelist D. L. Moody for the way he did evangelism. Moody replied, "I like my way of doing it better than your way of not doing it."[6]

Jesus said the laborers are few. A laborer is someone who gets out into the fields and goes to work. And yes, evangelism *is* work, difficult work. But as has been said, "Without God, man cannot. Without man, God will not."

At times evangelism doesn't seem worth the effort. But a farmer might feel the same way when a crop doesn't take, as might a fisherman when he doesn't get a single bite. But when your table is filled with food or when you reel in that record-setting fish, it all becomes worthwhile. When you see a person whom you've been praying for come to Christ, it's all worth it. The Bible says there is joy in heaven over one sinner who comes to repentance (Luke 15:7), and "those who sow in tears shall reap in joy. He who continually goes forth weeping, bearing seed for sowing, shall doubtless come again with rejoicing, bringing his sheaves with him" (Ps. 126:5–6).

The people are many, their needs are great, and God wants laborers. Note that Jesus said, "Therefore pray the Lord of the harvest to send out laborers into *His* harvest" (Luke 10:2). It is *His* harvest, not ours. Many of our attempts at sharing the gospel fail because we try to do it in our own strength. As I pointed out earlier, conversion is the work of God and God alone.

In the original language, the phrase *send out* is much more forceful. It means to "push them forward and thrust them out." So this verse could be translated, "Therefore pray the Lord of the harvest to *thrust out* laborers into His harvest."

Jesus used another important word in this verse: *pray.* We should pray for the Lord to raise up laborers for His harvest. But we must also be willing to become laborers ourselves. When we hold a Harvest Crusade event, hundreds of people volunteer to help, from ushers to counselors to prayer warriors asking God to bring people to the crusade. And that's only naming a few ways people labor in the harvest.

How about you? Is God thrusting you out among family and friends? Are you working in the field, or are you sitting in the shade drinking lemonade? The harvest is great, but the laborers are few. The observers are many. The critics are many. *But the laborers are few.*

God is looking for workers. He said, "I looked for a man among them who would build up the wall and stand before me in the gap on behalf of the land so I would not have to destroy it, but I found none" (Ezek. 22:30 NIV) and "for the eyes of the LORD range throughout the earth to strengthen those whose hearts are fully committed to him" (2 Chron. 16:9 NIV).

Will you pray that the Lord would send laborers to the harvest? Will you become a laborer yourself? Will you ask the Holy Spirit to move your heart to answer the desire and command of Jesus? Will you allow God's Spirit to stir you deeply with a burden for those who are like sheep without a shepherd?

If you pray for these things, He may call you to cross the ocean or simply cross the street. Regardless, He needs you to be a laborer in the harvest. We need to influence our culture and go into all the world to preach the gospel.

Before we do that, however, we need to know exactly *what* the gospel is. So let's look at the definition together in the next chapter.

————

The Three Ws of Evangelism

Who is called to "go into all the world"? *We are*. We have been redeemed by Jesus and belong to Him. As our Commander in Chief, He commands us to do this.

Where are we to go? *Everywhere*. We are to go into all our world and preach the gospel— in our neighborhoods, schools, beaches, malls ... everywhere.

Why are we to do this? *Because God has chosen to reach people through people.* Following Jesus' example, we need to genuinely care for non-Christians.

━━━━━

16

THE "WHAT" OF EVANGELISM:
THE GOSPEL

On May 15, 2006, British mountaineer David Sharp died near the summit of Mount Everest in a rocky cave. It was Sharp's third attempt to scale the world's highest mountain, and media reports speculated on whether he reached the top. But the irony of his tragic story is that while the blood in his arms and legs was turning to ice, a possible forty-two people passed Sharp that morning on their way to the summit—people who could have saved him. Some looked the other way, while a few paused long enough to hear him say, "My name is David Sharp. I'm with Asian Trekking ..." Upon hearing of Sharp's death, one climber coldheartedly remarked, "We know the risk. People die on Everest every year." When the media later picked up on comments by Sir Edmund Hillary, the first climber ever to summit Everest, he strongly criticized those who hadn't helped Sharp, reportedly calling their actions "despicable."[1] Before he left on his trip, Sharp had assured his mother, "You are never on your own. There are climbers everywhere."[2]

That tragedy on Everest sounds a lot like a modern version of Jesus' parable of the good samaritan. But it also sounds like some Christians, those who are so busy on their way up to the summit that they bypass non-Christians without so much as a twinge of concern. They watch them slowly die, or worse, never notice them to begin with.

Jesus always had time for individuals, patiently engaging, conversing, loving, and winning them to faith. All believers have been called to do the same.

So far, we've learned that Jesus gave us marching orders to "go into all the world and preach the good news to all creation" (Mark 16:15 NIV). Yet in all honesty, many—if not most—of us are not obeying His command. Why is that? I hear believers cite reasons such as feelings of inadequacy or lack of skill when it comes to sharing the gospel. Others are afraid of failure and how people will respond. Those are valid concerns, by the way. But in the pages that follow, I want to help you overcome those concerns and realize that God can and will use you to bring others into His kingdom. Granted, not every Christian is called as an evangelist, but we are all called *to evangelize*. We are called to share the gospel.

What Is the Gospel?

What is the gospel? What elements must it include for it to be accurate? Are there "false gospels" we must be aware of?

You might be thinking, *I'll leave that to you pastors and theologians to figure out. All I know is that I'm already saved and going to heaven.* But we all need to know the gospel for two very important reasons:

1. We want to make sure we have heard and responded to the true gospel, rather than have a false hope concerning a salvation we think we have. Our eternal destiny hangs on it.

2. Jesus commanded us to "go into all the world and preach the gospel." We cannot remain disengaged or disinterested in this subject, because the eternal destinies of many people hang in the balance.

Beware of Counterfeits

What would you think of a surgeon who just started cutting away on a patient without really knowing what he or she was doing? One mistake and the patient could be disabled for life or even killed. The message we bring has even more far-reaching consequences than these, because there are eternal ramifications.

Yet so many carelessly offer God's forgiveness without any mention of repentance. Or perhaps some will present Jesus Christ as a mere additive to make one's life a little better and more successful. This is not the true gospel, and it can give false hope.

On the other extreme, some offer a rule-laden or over-complex gospel by telling people they must do certain things or look a certain way to be saved. This robs the gospel of its simplicity and power—and imposes false guilt.

This is why the Bible reminds us that we as Christians are to rightly divide the word of truth (2 Tim. 2:15). It also tells us "Watch your life and doctrine closely. Persevere in them, because if you do, you will save both yourself and your hearers" (1 Tim. 4:16 NIV).

Some Christians might say, "I'm not into doctrine. I just love Jesus!" That is a sweet sentiment, but Christians who embrace it might end up loving *the wrong Jesus.*

C. S. Lewis gave this warning: "If you do not listen to theology, that will not mean that you have no ideas about God. It will mean that you have a lot of wrong ones—bad, muddled, out-of-date ideas."[3]

Therefore, we must be careful to accurately present the whole gospel, because there are also false, counterfeit gospels. Paul wrote to the churches of Galatia,

> I am astonished that you are so quickly deserting the one who called you by the grace of Christ and are turning to a different gospel—which is really no gospel at all. Evidently some people are throwing you into confusion and are trying to pervert the gospel of Christ. But even if we or an angel from heaven should preach a gospel other than the one we preached to you, let him be eternally condemned! (Gal. 1:6–8 NIV)

The Good News and the Bad News

So together let's explore the necessary elements of the gospel. A technical definition of the word *gospel* is "good news." We've all heard the expression "I have some good news and some bad news." When it comes to sharing the gospel, we must present both the good news and the bad news.

The bad news is the fact that we all stand as sinners before a holy God. No matter who we are, *we have all sinned*—sometimes in ignorance and often on purpose. The Bible tells us that "all have sinned and fall short of the glory of God" (Rom. 3:23) and that "if we say that we have no sin, we deceive ourselves, and the truth is not in us" (1 John 1:8). God gave us His law, the Ten Commandments, not to make us righteous but to show us that we all fall miserably short. These commandments act as a moral mirror showing us our flaws and sin. They shut our mouths and open our eyes.

Often when I share the gospel, I go over a few of the Ten Commandments and ask, "Have you ever broken any of these commandments? Have you ever stolen, lied, or taken God's name in vain? The Bible says, 'For whoever keeps the whole law and yet stumbles at just one point is guilty of breaking all of it'" (James 2:10 NIV). This verse shows that everyone needs Jesus. Everyone has sinned, and no one is good enough to get into heaven.

Yet the idea of humanity's utter sinfulness is difficult for many people to stomach. Some believe in the innate goodness of man. But as the Scripture says, "God looks down from heaven upon the children of men, to see if there are any who understand, who seek God. Every one of them has turned aside; they have together become corrupt; there is none who does good, no, not one" (Ps. 53:2–3).

This does not mean humanity isn't capable of commendable things. Some people are great humanitarians or heroes. The soldier who throws himself on a grenade to protect his buddies is a great hero. A person who helps the hurting is good in the sense of human kindness. So to say, "There is none who does good, no, not one," does not mean there is no good in people, but that there is no good in people that can satisfy God.

God is holy, and He requires holiness from us. Hebrews 12:14 tells us, "Make every effort to live in peace with all men and to be holy; without holiness no one will see the Lord" (NIV). And we are told in 1 Peter 1:15–16, "But just as he who called you is holy, so be holy in all you do; for it is written: 'Be holy, because I am holy'" (NIV).

I read about a man named Fred Turner who, a number of years ago, decided to walk across America to prove that most people are good. He made it through only one state before he was robbed and pushed off a bridge.

According to Turner, a faded red pickup truck pulled next to him while he was walking across a bridge. "They asked me if I was the guy walking across America," he said. "I told them yes, and they said, 'Good. Give me your wallet.'" Then they pushed him. He dropped off the bridge, falling seventy-five to one hundred feet.[4]

Only One Resolution

Humanity is not basically good; we are basically bad. *Very bad.* But just as a jeweler will display a beautiful ring or necklace against a dark velvet background to accentuate its beauty, God seeks to show us how good the gospel is by first sharing the bad news. Seeing our complete weakness, our inability to do anything to alleviate our miserable condition, God did the ultimate for us:

> When we were utterly helpless, Christ came at just
> the right time and died for us sinners. Now, most
> people would not be willing to die for an upright

person, though someone might perhaps be willing
to die for a person who is especially good. But God
showed his great love for us by sending Christ to die
for us while we were still sinners. (Rom. 5:6–8 NLT)

Because there was no other way to satisfy the righteous demands
of God, because of our inability to improve ourselves (much less save
ourselves), because we faced a future in hell because of our sin, God,
in His great love, sent His own Son to come down from heaven and
die on the cross in our place. Paul personalized this great act of mercy
by saying, "I have been crucified with Christ and I no longer live, but
Christ lives in me. The life I live in the body, I live by faith in the
Son of God, who loved me and gave himself for me" (Gal. 2:20 NIV).

There was no other way to resolve the sin issue we all face. We
know that God is perfect. We know that humanity is imperfect
and sinful. So Jesus, the God-Man, bridged the gap between sinful humanity and a holy God. As 2 Corinthians 5:18–19 tells us,

And all of this is a gift from God, who brought us
back to himself through Christ. And God has given
us this task of reconciling people to him. For God was
in Christ, reconciling the world to himself, no longer
counting people's sins against them. And he gave us
this wonderful message of reconciliation. (NLT)

It's not about what we did to please or reach God. We did everything to displease Him and failed to reach Him. Instead, "all of this
is a gift from God, who brought us back to himself through Christ."

This is why Jesus Christ is the only way to the Father. Jesus Himself said it: "I am the way, the truth, and the life. No one comes to the Father except through Me" (John 14:6).

Peter echoed those words as he stood before the Sanhedrin: "Nor is there salvation in any other, for there is no other name under heaven given among men by which we must be saved" (Acts 4:12). Paul said the same thing: "For there is one God and one Mediator between God and men, the Man Christ Jesus" (1 Tim. 2:5). For us as Christians to say anything else would be wrong—and it would be a misrepresentation of the gospel.

There on the cross, all the sin of the world was poured upon Jesus Christ as He became the sin sacrifice for us: "God made him who had no sin to be sin for us, so that in him we might become the righteousness of God" (2 Cor. 5:21 NIV). At the cross, Jesus paid the penalty for every sin we have ever committed.

In the movie *The Last Emperor,* a young child is anointed as the last emperor of China. This child lives a life of incredible luxury with one thousand servants at his command. One day his brother asks him, "What happens when you do wrong?"

"When I do wrong," the boy emperor responds, "someone else is punished." To demonstrate, he breaks a jar, and one of his servants is beaten.[5] In the gospel, the very opposite is true. Jesus reversed that ancient pattern: When the servants sinned, the King was punished. Grace is free only because the Giver Himself has borne the cost.

The Essential Gospel Message

In 1 Corinthians 15:1–4, Paul gives a simple summation of the gospel:

Now, brothers, I want to remind you of *the gospel I preached to you,* which you received and on which you have taken your stand. *By this gospel you are saved,* if you hold firmly to the word I preached to you. Otherwise, you have believed in vain.

For what I received I passed on to you as of first importance: that *Christ died for our sins* according to the Scriptures, that *he was buried,* that *he was raised on the third day according to the Scriptures.* (NIV)

The gospel, in a nutshell, is this: Christ died for our sins, was buried, and was raised on the third day. *Imbed that sentence deep into your mind.* There are other elements to the gospel, but this is the cornerstone—the death and resurrection of Jesus Christ. Someone once asked C. H. Spurgeon if he could put his Christian faith into a few words. He answered, "It is all in four words: Jesus died for me."[6]

Consider the fact that the apostle Paul was a brilliant orator and communicator. He studied both biblical law and the wisdom literature of Greece. If anyone could have leaned on his intellect to share the gospel, it would have been Paul. Yet it's amazing to read accounts in the book of Acts of his sharing the gospel—Paul kept it simple. He emphasized the importance of simplicity in his writings:

For Christ did not send me to baptize, but to preach the gospel—not with words of human wisdom, lest the cross of Christ be emptied of its power. (1 Cor. 1:17 NIV)

When I came to you, brothers, I did not come with eloquence or superior wisdom as I proclaimed to you the testimony about God. For I resolved to know nothing while I was with you except Jesus Christ and him crucified. (1 Cor. 2:1–2 NIV)

Typically, Paul began with his personal testimony. Then he spoke about what happened when Jesus died on the cross. This is a pattern that we can follow.

Of course, non-Christians often fire off hard questions. But we need to know that the essence of the gospel message is the cross. The information I've just shared is enough to make you spiritually dangerous; it will enable you to make an impact for the kingdom of God.

We often underestimate the raw power of the gospel to reach even the most hardened heart. Yet remember what Paul said, "For the message of the cross is foolishness to those who are perishing, but to us who are being saved it is the power of God" (1 Cor. 1:18 NIV), and "I am not ashamed of the gospel of Christ, for it is the power of God to salvation for everyone who believes" (Rom. 1:16). Paul reminded us that there is a distinct power in the simple message of the life, death, and resurrection of Jesus Christ.

So don't underestimate the gospel's broad appeal. Let us not be ashamed of its simplicity. We can't add to it or take away from it. We can only proclaim it and stand back and watch what God will do.

I've been preaching the gospel for more than three decades now, and I am amazed time and time again by how God powerfully uses this simple yet incredibly profound message. He radically changes the lives of everyone from satanists to religious people, from broken families and drug addicts to those deceived by cults.

Praise God for the gospel!

The Conversion Process

What is the appropriate response to the gospel? How do we enter into a relationship with God? Matthew 11:28–30 provides the answer: "Come to Me, all you who labor and are heavy laden, and I will give you rest. Take My yoke upon you and learn from Me, for I am gentle and lowly in heart, and you will find rest for your souls. For My yoke is easy and My burden is light."

In these verses, Jesus gives us three steps that define the process of entering into and enjoying a relationship with God:

1. Come to Me.
2. Take My yoke upon you.
3. Learn from Me.

First, we must come to Him. We come to Him with all our problems, sins, and shortcomings. We respond to His invitation with the assurance that He said, "All that the Father gives me will come to me, and whoever comes to me I will never drive away" (John 6:37 NIV). Conversion is not a long, drawn-out process. It is immediate and instantaneous. Thinking about it is not enough. When the prodigal son was in a distant country, he knew he needed to return home. But thinking about it and doing it are two different things. That's why, whenever we share the gospel, we should always give people the opportunity to *come to Christ.* Much evangelism doesn't get a big reaction, *because we don't throw the net!*

Of course, there is a right time and a wrong time to throw the net. First, we want to make sure the people we're talking with understand the essential gospel message. They need to understand that to come to Christ, they must receive Him as both Lord and Savior. They must confess and turn from their sin, as 1 John 1:9 says: "If we confess our sins, he is faithful and just and will forgive us our sins and purify us from all unrighteousness" (NIV). Finally, they must believe in Jesus, as John 3:16 says: "For God so loved the world that He gave His only begotten Son, that whoever *believes in Him* should not perish but have everlasting life."

The Role of Repentance

The second step in the conversion process is "take My yoke upon you." People of Jesus' day readily understood this phrase, but it's largely lost on us.

The idea of being "yoked" to Jesus means that we surrender to His direction for our lives. There's no such thing as having Christ as Savior *but not as Lord.* We must give Him the steering wheel of our lives, so to speak. My family could tell you that I am the worst backseat driver. I like to be in control of the car. But Jesus says to us, "I want the steering wheel, and I don't need your advice."

Many of us have our own plans for our lives and we ask the Lord to come along for the ride. Some people may even have a little bumper sticker on their cars that says, "God is my copilot." *But God does not want to be their copilot!* In fact, He doesn't even want anyone else in the cockpit. Jesus wants to control our lives, and that is actually a wonderful thing.

Imagine being in a car that is careening out of control, when NASCAR driver Jeff Gordon offers to take the wheel. Even with my strong tendency toward backseat driving, I would gladly let him drive. Why? Because I know the odds of getting control of that car are much better with him behind the wheel.

Jesus offers to take control of our lives by allowing us to take His yoke upon us. First, we must admit that we are helpless sinners in desperate need of a Savior. In the process, we turn away from our old, sinful lifestyles and are willing to change and become different people. In short, we need to repent. Peter preached, "Repent, then, and turn to God, so that your sins may be wiped out, that times of refreshing may come from the Lord" (Acts 3:19 NIV).

Belief and repentance are two sides of the same coin. To believe is to take hold of something, and to repent is to let go of something. Paul brought both ideas together in Acts 20:21: "I have declared to both Jews and Greeks that they must turn to God in repentance and have faith in our Lord Jesus" (NIV).

Repentance means more than merely feeling regret or sorrow. We may feel sorry for sin, especially if we reap the consequences. The person caught in a lie is sorry. The criminal who gets caught is sorry. The teenage girl who finds out she's pregnant outside of marriage is sorry. But does this sorrow lead to change? Not if the person caught in a lie determines to be more careful next time. Not if the criminal plots his next crime with more foresight. Not if the teenage girl will try to have only "safe sex" from now on.

Repentance means a change of mind and heart, and a sincere confession of wrongdoing. To repent means to turn around, to change one's direction, and to change both the mind and will.

The recognition of personal sin is the first step in repentance. But stopping there can be useless at best and dangerous at worst. An insincere King Saul confessed his sin (1 Sam. 15:24), but that didn't stop him from his collision course with judgment. The rich young ruler who asked Jesus how to have eternal life left sorrowful, but not repentant (Luke 18:23). Even Judas Iscariot felt sad over his betrayal of Jesus (Matt. 27:4). All of these men recognized their sin, yet none of them repented.

Paul put it succinctly when he shared Jesus' words about salvation: "To *open their eyes,* in order to *turn them from darkness to light,* and *from the power of Satan to God,* that they may *receive forgiveness of sins and an inheritance* among those who are sanctified by faith in Me" (Acts 26:18).

When I am preaching, I often sum up my messages with the following points:

1. Realize you are a sinner.
2. Recognize Christ died for you.
3. Repent of your sins.
4. Receive Christ as Savior and Lord.

Becoming New

Here's what we've learned of the conversion process: First, we must come to Him. Then we must take His yoke upon us. The next step in the process is to *learn from Him*. As we walk and talk with Jesus Christ in our hearts and lives and begin to read His Word, we will see things with new eyes, because we are new people.

The only way to know whether a conversion has taken place is to look for results. Two of those results will be a hatred for sin and a love for God's Word. In 1 John, we find four earmarks of a true conversion.

Confession of Jesus as Lord: "Whoever confesses that Jesus is the Son of God, God abides in him, and he in God" (1 John 4:15).

Unhappiness or misery over personal sin: "No one who is born of God will continue to sin, because God's seed remains in him; he cannot go on sinning, because he has been born of God" (1 John 3:9 NIV). From the original language, the phrase *will continue to sin* could be translated "habitually sin."

Fellowship with other believers: "Everyone who believes that Jesus is the Christ is born of God, and everyone who loves the father loves his child as well" (1 John 5:1 NIV). And "These people left our churches, but they never really belonged with us; otherwise they would have stayed with us. When they left, it proved that they did not belong with us" (1 John 2:19 NLT).

Obedience to Christ's commands: "This is love for God: to obey his commands. And his commands are not burdensome" (1 John 5:3 NIV).

How Will They Hear?

One of His commands, we've learned so far, is to "go into all the world and preach the gospel." My question for you is this: When was the last time you told someone about Jesus Christ? Again, as Romans 10:14

says, "How, then, can they call on the one they have not believed in? And how can they believe in the one of whom they have not heard? And how can they hear without someone preaching to them?" (NIV).

There are people right now waiting for you, *Christian,* to show them the way. As we make our way up the summit, let's not forget those along the way, those people waiting for someone to help them with the only message that can change their eternal destiny: *the gospel of Jesus Christ.*

Will you do that? Will you be available for God to use you?

——————

The Essential Gospel

Christ died for our sins, was buried, and was raised on the third day.

——————

17

PRACTICAL EFFECTS
OF SALVATION

As we seek to share the gospel message with others, there are some biblical concepts we need to grasp before we get the bigger picture.

Two key terms we must know and understand are *justification* and *sanctification*. Understanding these terms can and will impact your Christian experience profoundly. So don't let these words put you off. You need to know what they mean and how they practically apply to you. These are the results of conversion.

Justification

C. H. Spurgeon said, "It is admitted by all evangelical Christians that the standing or falling in the church is that of justification by faith."[1] So what does it mean to be "justified" before God?

The word *justified* carries a twofold meaning. First, this word means to be forgiven of all sin. Have you done anything of which you are ashamed? If you repent of that sin and turn your back on it, the Bible clearly declares that you are forgiven.

Have you ever lost anything in a lake or the ocean? Once it goes down, it goes way down. God takes our sins and throws them into the deepest part of the sea. Simply put, our sins are gone. Therefore, we should not choose to remember what God has chosen to forget. As Corrie ten Boom once said, God takes our sins, "casts them into the depths of the sea, forgiven and forgotten. Then He puts out a sign, NO FISHING ALLOWED."[2]

But forgiveness is only one part of justification. If justification were only forgiveness, I would say that it's the greatest deal ever offered to humanity. But justification also speaks of something far greater: what God has put in its place. The word *justified* means to have something placed to your credit. The Greek word describing this process is used eleven times in Romans 4. It is translated by the English verbs *account,* or *count.* Romans 4:5 tells us, "But to him who does not work but believes on Him who justifies the ungodly, *his faith is accounted for righteousness.*"

So we see that justification is both God's removal of our guilt and condemnation through forgiveness, and what God has given us in their place. Justification is a legal act of God, declaring the sinner guiltless. It is a complete acquittal. When God justifies us, He does so by placing the righteousness of Christ into our accounts. That balances the moral and spiritual debt against us. As Paul said, "I no longer count on my own righteousness through obeying the law; rather, I become righteous through faith in Christ. For God's way of making us right with himself depends on faith" (Phil. 3:9 NLT).

This is not a gradual process. It is instantaneous. It is immediate. That is what God did for you through justification. He forgave you of all of your wrongs. He removed your sins. And He put Christ's righteousness into your account.

Sanctification

Having experienced justification, we will also experience sanctification. Sanctification means being "set apart." That is, set apart to be used by God and to become more like Christ:

> In a large house there are articles not only of gold and silver, but also of wood and clay; some are for noble purposes and some for ignoble. If a man cleanses himself from the latter, he will be an instrument for noble purposes, *made holy,* useful to the Master and prepared to do any good work. (2 Tim. 2:20–21 NIV)

Sanctification is a part of the process of the new birth. A note in D. L. Moody's Bible used seven words to describe the sanctified life:

1. Justification—a change of state, a new standing before God.
2. Repentance—a change of mind, a new mind about God.
3. Regeneration—a change of nature, a new heart from God.
4. Conversion—a change of life, a new life for God.

5. Adoption—a change of family, a new relationship toward God.

6. Sanctification—a change of service, separation unto God.

7. Glorification—a change of condition, at home with God.[3]

A License to Sin?

So, now that we've learned what God did for us through justification and sanctification, this brings us to this question: Can you be a genuine child of God, yet continue to live a sinful lifestyle?

In Romans 6, Paul anticipated and refuted a similar idea when talking to the religious leaders of his day. They thought because he was teaching that salvation comes totally and completely from God, that there is nothing we can do to earn it, then it stands to reason that we can go on sinning. After all, won't God forgive us?

Obviously, this isn't what Paul taught. One thing we often forget is that although there is forgiveness of sin, there are still repercussions. We sometimes confuse God's grace with God's approval, and we believe that somehow God doesn't mind our sin. When a believer sins, but truly repents, there can still be very grave ramifications.

This was certainly the case with David. After he confessed to committing murder to cover up his adultery with Bathsheba, the prophet Nathan said to him, "The LORD also has put away your sin; you shall not die. However, because by this deed you have given great occasion to the enemies of the LORD to blaspheme, the child also who is born to you shall surely die" (2 Sam. 12:13–14).

Scripture is clear about this: "Do not be deceived: God cannot be mocked. A man reaps what he sows" (Gal. 6:7 NIV). For example, if you robbed a bank, got caught by the authorities, and then repented before God and said, "I'm sorry," God would forgive you. But you still would go to jail.

The problem with the religious people of Paul's day was that they put the cart before the horse. They believed that holy living, which to them meant keeping to the rules, brought about God's favor and therefore resulted in salvation. But Paul showed that because of the extensiveness of our sinful condition, there was no way we could *earn* God's approval. We all fail miserably and continually.

God's favor toward us comes not on the basis of what we've done for Him, but on what He's done for us. So holy living (which we are incapable of) will not produce salvation. *But salvation will produce holy living.*

Therefore the teaching of justification is not a license to sin, but an incentive to obey. "No one who is born of God will continue to sin, because God's seed remains in him; he cannot go on sinning, because he has been born of God" (1 John 3:9 NIV).

In Romans 6, the repetition of the word *know* in verses 6 and 9 indicates that Paul wanted us to understand a basic doctrine:

> For we *know* that our old self was crucified with him so that the body of sin might be done away with, that we should no longer be slaves to sin.... For we *know* that since Christ was raised from the dead, he cannot die again; death no longer has mastery over him. (NIV)

Many would think the way to overcome sin is to say, "No! No!" But Paul's method for overcoming it was by teaching, "Know! Know!" Christian living depends on Christian learning. Duty is always founded on doctrine. If Satan can keep Christians ignorant, he can keep them impotent. We are often defeated in day-to-day living because we do not fully realize how much God placed in our spiritual bank accounts. This is like trying to hold back the enemy in a battle without using any ammunition, while all the time having a massive stockpile that sits unused. Our defeat lies largely in our ignorance of the facts.

Jesus Christ gives the power to live a new life free of sin's control. That power is not the result of imitation. We cannot avoid sin by merely imitating Christ. Nor does the power come from repeating certain phrases or prayers. The power comes not through imitation, but impartation.

This is a revolutionary concept. It's not trying to humanly live a divine life, but to divinely live a human life. It is appropriating the divine provisions that God gave us. It is finding and using the ammunition. It is taking hold of our possessions, just as the children of Israel had to take possession of their land:

> Moses My servant is dead. Now therefore, arise, go over this Jordan, you and all this people, to the land which I am giving to them—the children of Israel. Every place that the sole of your foot will tread upon I have given you, as I said to Moses. From the wilderness and this Lebanon as far as the great river, the River Euphrates, all the land of the Hittites, and

> to the Great Sea toward the going down of the sun,
>
> shall be your territory. (Josh. 1:2–4)

The land was theirs, but they still had to take possession of it. In the same way, we can stand around and admire these principles of justification and sanctification, thinking, *Isn't it great what God has given to us?* But do we put them into practice? The answer, many times, is no.

Justification by faith is not simply a legal matter between God and His people; rather, it is a living relationship. It is justification that brings us life (Rom. 5:18). We are in Christ, and we are identified with Him. Therefore, whatever happened to Christ, happened to us. *When He died, we died. When He rose, we rose with Him.* And we are now seated in "heavenly places" with Him as well (Eph. 2:6).

Because of this living union with Jesus, we also have a totally different relationship to sin. Many times when believers "pray for victory," they are missing an essential truth that could revolutionize their spiritual lives: We don't fight *for* victory; we fight *from* a place of victory. So we don't fight the devil in our own strength. We stand in the Lord and in the power of His might. We share in what He has already done on our behalf. We stand in the finished work of the cross.

The Choice Is Ours

So the question arises: "Shall we continue in sin that grace may abound?" (Rom. 6:1). In the original language, the word *continue* carries the idea of habitual persistence. This word was sometimes used to describe a person purposely living in a certain place and making it his permanent residence.

One summer, I had the opportunity to spend a few days with my family in Nantucket, a beautiful place off the east coast of the United States. I had never visited anywhere quite like it. We especially enjoyed walking along, looking at the different houses. To provide a sense of continuity and uniformity on the island, there are only five shades of paint that people can use on their homes, all of which appear basically gray. There is dark gray, medium gray, and light gray.

As my son Jonathan and I took pictures, we found one dilapidated house, built partly over the water. Nets hung off the walls and someone had piled junk here and there. The windows were broken, and the front door hung by one hinge. I thought this house would make a great photo.

And I was certain no one lived there. So I climbed up on the little deck, steadied myself, and told Jonathan to take a picture. Then I went into the house and popped out the doorway. Just as Jonathan readied to take the next shot, a woman in the back of the house yelled at me and told me to get out! I have to admit, she gave me quite a start, and we got out of there quickly. I couldn't believe someone actually lived in this place. For that matter, I couldn't believe anyone would be allowed to live there, because it looked like the house could come crashing down at any moment.

This event reminded me of how people purposely live in a state of sin. That woman chose to live in this dangerous environment, just as some people choose to live in sin. Paul asked how those whose relationship to sin has been broken by Jesus can still walk and live in sin. That should be our past, not our present. As Paul wrote to the believers in Ephesus,

> As for you, you were dead in your transgressions and sins, in which you used to live when you followed the ways of this world and of the ruler of the kingdom of the air, the spirit who is now at work in those who are disobedient. All of us also lived among them at one time, gratifying the cravings of our sinful nature and following its desires and thoughts. Like the rest, we were by nature objects of wrath. (Eph. 2:1–3 NIV)

The word *ways* in verse 2 was used for a weathervane that blows whatever way the wind does. We once "followed the ways of this world," Paul said, but now that has all changed. Now we are "a new creation; the old has gone, the new has come!" (2 Cor 5:17 NIV).

That is not to say we won't struggle with sin and temptation to some degree throughout the Christian life. The Bible clearly points out, "If we claim to be without sin, we deceive ourselves and the truth is not in us" (1 John 1:8 NIV). When Paul asked, "Shall we continue in sin that grace may abound?" he was not speaking of an occasional falling into sin, because that happens to every believer. Paul spoke of intentional, willful sinning as an established pattern of life.

However, if there's been no change in a person's lifestyle *after* conversion, and if he or she continues in sin, the question is not so much whether that person can lose salvation, but whether that person ever truly converted in the first place. Perhaps he or she never really heard the true gospel. I would suggest that many who claim to be Christians really are not. They never turned "from darkness to light, and from the power of Satan to God" (Acts 26:18). Commentator Donald Grey Barnhouse said, "Holiness starts where justification finishes, and if holiness does not start, we have the right to suspect that justification never started either."[4]

Paul's answer to the question of whether we should continue in sin was "Certainly not! How shall we who died to sin live any longer in it?" (Rom. 6:2). In this verse, he refers to our position in Christ. Just as Jesus was crucified and then rose again from the dead, we have gone through the same thing because we are in Him. We are dead to sin. In other words, when Jesus died to sin, we died to sin.

Paul went on to illustrate this idea:

> Or do you not know that as many of us as were baptized into Christ Jesus were baptized into His death? Therefore we were buried with Him through baptism into death, that just as Christ was raised from the dead by the glory of the Father, even so we also should walk in newness of life. (Rom. 6:3–4)

We as believers have made a break with the past. We are dead and buried through our identification with the death and burial of Jesus Christ.

What Baptism Means

We have a symbol of our identification with Christ in water baptism. Many misunderstand the meaning and purpose of baptism.

Water baptism is an outward *showing* of an inward *doing,* just as wearing a wedding ring is an outward symbol of what happened on that person's wedding day. Baptism does not wash away one's sins any more than simply putting on a wedding ring makes one married. Baptism is a symbol of identifying with the death and resurrection of Jesus Christ. Some think baptism is a ritual that plays a role in salvation, which is why they will have their babies baptized as a type of dedication. I am all for infant dedication, but I am not for infant baptism. Why? Because there's no precedent for it in Scripture.

Two requirements are necessary to make baptism meaningful.

Repentance. We must repent. Peter told those present at Pentecost, "Repent and be baptized, every one of you, in the name of Jesus Christ for the forgiveness of your sins" (Acts 2:38 NIV).

Belief in the Lord Jesus Christ. We must believe in Jesus Christ as the Son of God. When Philip talked with the Ethiopian eunuch on the road from Jerusalem to Gaza, the eunuch said, "'See, here is water. What hinders me from being baptized?' Then Philip said, 'If you believe with all your heart, you may.' And he answered and said, 'I believe that Jesus Christ is the Son of God'" (Acts 8:36–37). So they went down into the water, and Philip baptized him.

Baptism represents saying good-bye to your old life. Paul raised the question, "Or don't you know that all of us who were baptized into Christ Jesus were baptized into his death?" (Rom. 6:3 NIV). So in a way, baptism is the only truly happy funeral service you ever attend. I read about a chaplain during Operation Desert Storm who had to come up with an alternative for baptizing the many American soldiers who came to Christ and asked to be baptized. Because there was no body of water available in the desert, the chaplain baptized the soldiers in a coffin filled with water. In all reality, it was a more-than-appropriate way to baptize, due to its symbolism.

So does a person have to be baptized to be saved? No. But if a person is saved, then he or she certainly should be baptized. The Bible commands us to do this, and as we've seen, it's even a part of the Great Commission: "Therefore go and make disciples of all nations, *baptizing* them in the name of the Father and of the Son and of the Holy Spirit" (Matt. 28:19).

But as important as baptism is, it is not a prerequisite for salvation. Some proponents of an idea called "baptismal regeneration" cite Mark 16:16, which says, "Whoever believes and is baptized will be saved, but whoever does not believe will be condemned" (NIV). But notice this verse does *not* say "he who does not believe and is not baptized will be condemned." The emphasis in that verse is on *believing* and on what should naturally follow. The emphasis is not on baptism.

If baptism were a requirement for salvation, then what about the thief on the cross who said to Jesus, "Lord, remember me when You come into Your kingdom"? Jesus didn't insist that the man be baptized. Instead, Jesus told him, "Assuredly, I say to you, today you will be with Me in Paradise" (Luke 23:42–43).

When Peter preached the gospel to some Gentiles and the Holy Spirit came upon them, Peter asked, "Can anyone keep these people from being baptized with water? They have received the Holy Spirit just as we have" (Acts 10:47 NIV). Clearly these people already believed and the Holy Spirit empowered them *before* they were baptized.

A New Beginning

Baptism is a symbol of new life in Christ, and the Bible is full of descriptions of the believer's new spiritual life. In Ezekiel, God promises a new heart: "I will give you a new heart and put a new spirit in you; I will remove from you your heart of stone and give you a heart of flesh" (Ezek. 36:26 NIV).

And Ephesians emphasizes a new nature: "Throw off your old sinful nature and your former way of life, which is corrupted by lust and deception. Instead, let the Spirit renew your thoughts and attitudes. Put on your new nature, created to be like God—truly righteous and holy" (Eph. 4:22–24 NLT).

Even though we should walk in the newness of life, as Paul pointed out, it's important to understand that we all still have the capacity to sin. The point is that we no longer live under the *jurisdiction* of sin. The power sin once had over us has been canceled. We don't have to sin. The tyranny and penalty of sin in every Christian's life has been broken, but sin's potential for expression in his or her life is still there. Christ died not only to destroy the penalty of past sin but also to cancel out the power of present sin.

Inner Turmoil

Even so, our human weakness makes us capable of giving in to the devil's temptations, especially when we live apart from the Holy Spirit's power and God's Word.

A man once compared his new and old natures to two dogs that ceaselessly scrap and fight against one another. He said, "My new nature and old nature are like two dogs that are constantly fighting, but I decide which dog will win."

"How do you decide?" someone asked.

"The one I want to win," he said, "I feed the most."

We all have a new nature and an old nature that are constantly battling. Which one will win? You decide by the one you feed the most. By neglecting the things of the Spirit, the potential for sin will become stronger with every passing day.

Doing Our Part

Paul said, "In the same way, count yourselves dead to sin but alive to God in Christ Jesus" (Rom. 6:11 NIV). God opened the prison door, but we must walk through it. There are certain things that only God can do and certain things that only we can do. Only God can justify. Only God can forgive. But on the other hand, only we can repent. And only we can appropriate and count these things as true in our lives—and take hold of our spiritual possessions.

Sin is a horrible master, and it finds a willing servant in the human body. The human body itself is neutral; it can be controlled by sin or by God. But the old nature gives sin a beachhead from which it can attack and control. Paul, lamenting this problem, said, "I know that nothing good lives in me, that is, in my sinful nature. For I have the desire to do what is good, but I cannot carry it out" (Rom. 7:18 NIV).

But an important truth emerges: "knowing this, that our old man was crucified with Him, that the body of sin might be done away with, that we should no longer be slaves of sin" (Rom. 6:6). The "old man," basically our old self, was crucified with Christ so that the body need not be controlled by sin. The phrase *done away with* does not mean "annihilated." It means "rendered inactive," "made of no effect," or simply "put out of business."

But sin wants to be our master. God could see this sinful bent in Cain before he killed Abel: "So the LORD said to Cain, 'Why are you angry? And why has your countenance fallen? If you do well, will you not be accepted? And if you do not do well, sin lies at the door. And its desire is for you, but you should rule over it'" (Gen. 4:6–7). The phrase *sin lies at the door* could be literally translated, "sin is crouching at your door." Clearly Cain struggled up to this point. God gave Cain a warning. In Cain's refusal to come to God on His terms, he flirted with disaster. The cause of his anger was sin, and sin later mastered him.

Sin is crouching at our doors too. For some of us, it has already crossed the threshold. So what can we do? How can we protect ourselves from the power of the devil and his forces?

First, we must realize that we cannot do it ourselves. Jesus told the story of a man possessed by a demon, but the demon was driven out. So the demon went and found seven other more wicked demons and they all returned and possessed the man again. Jesus said, "The last state of that man is worse than the first" (Matt. 12:45). The only defense against sin crouching at our doors is Jesus Christ Himself. When the devil knocks at your door, it's a good idea to say, "Lord, would You mind getting that?"

Know, Reckon, Yield

Jesus asked a man who was sick for thirty-eight years, "Do you want to get well?" (John 5:6 NIV). We must ask ourselves this same question, because many people do not. In getting well, there's God's part, and there's our part. The question is, do we really want to be free from sin? And if so, what should we do?

Three words from Romans 6 put it all together for us: *know, reckon,* and *yield. Know* centers in the mind, *reckon* focuses on the heart, and *yield* touches on the will.

First, we must *know.* This aspect of getting free from sin deals primarily with the mind. For us as believers to live out the fullness of our new lives in Jesus Christ, for us to truly live as the new creations that we are, we must *know* that we aren't what we used to be. We must understand that we're not remodeled sinners *but remade saints.* We must understand that despite our present conflict with sin, we're no longer under sin's control. This is clearly something the devil doesn't want us to know.

Second, we must *reckon.* This aspect of getting free from sin deals primarily with the heart. "Likewise you also, reckon yourselves to be dead indeed to sin, but alive to God in Christ Jesus our Lord" (Rom. 6:11). In some parts of our nation, especially many Southern states, *reckon* means "to think" or "to guess." But the biblical use of the word is different altogether. And it is very important for us to understand. It means "to count," "to take into account," "to calculate," and "to put to one's account and count as true." Paul was saying that we need to act on God's Word and *count it as true* for ourselves.

Reckoning is not acting *as if* it were so; it is acting *because* it is so. Reckoning is not claiming a promise in faith, but acting on a fact. God does not command us to be dead to sin; He tells us that we are dead to sin and alive to God—and then He commands us to act on it. Even if we do not act on it, the facts are still true. Being dead to sin is only half the story. Our victory is not in our deadness to sin alone, but also in our being alive to God. The death to sin is negative, while our life in God is positive. The one side removes penalty, while the other side gives power.

Third, we must *yield*. This aspect of becoming free from sin deals primarily with the will. "And do not present your members as instruments of unrighteousness to sin, but present yourselves to God as being alive from the dead, and your members as instruments of righteousness to God" (Rom. 6:13). The word *present* could also be translated "yield," which means to "place at one's disposal, to offer as a sacrifice." The same word is used again in Romans 12:1, where we are told to "present [our] bodies a living sacrifice." This is an act of the will, based on our knowledge of what Christ has done for us. Yielding ourselves to God is an intelligent action—not an impulsive, momentary decision based on mere emotional stirring.

It's also important to notice the verb tenses in Romans 6:13. One translation of this verse reads,

> Do not continue offering or yielding your bodily members [and faculties] to sin as instruments (tools) of wickedness. But offer and yield yourselves to God as though you have been raised from the dead to [perpetual] life, and your bodily members [and faculties] to God, presenting them as implements of righteousness. (AB)

What Will It Be?

Sin has no power to control a believer unless the believer chooses to obey its lusts. Every day, we make a choice about who or what will control us. When you get up tomorrow, you can occupy your mind with the things of God or fill it with useless clutter—*or worse, with sinful things*. You can spend your time using your lips to glorify God and build up the people around you, or you can engage in slander, gossip, or other things dishonoring to the Lord. There are so many choices that you will make.

God gave you the resources for the life He wants you to live. Now is the time for you to know what they are, to count them as true in your own life, and then to yield all of yourself to Him.

The Results of Conversion

Justification is a legal act of God, declaring the sinner guiltless before Him. It is a complete acquittal. When God justifies us, He forgives totally, and He also places the righteousness of Christ into our account.

Sanctification means being "set apart." That is, set apart to be used by God and to become more like Christ.

18

WHAT'S YOUR STORY?

I love a good story, especially a true story about a real person. When I go on vacation and take along books to read, I generally don't choose fiction. I prefer biographies. I'm always interested in biographies of different people from all different walks of life. And I am as interested in their failures as in their successes. I want to know what makes them tick and what they went through in their lives. The stories of people have always interested me.

When it comes to sharing your faith, one of the most effective tools in your evangelistic toolbox is your personal testimony. Your testimony is a bridge-builder. It is a way to connect with people so they can see why you believe what you believe. Your testimony can help others see how they can come to faith as well. It's also a great way to engage a person.

Through sharing your testimony, you inadvertently preach the gospel. Instead of abruptly saying, "You are a sinner. You need to repent," you can share the gospel indirectly. You can say something like, "You know, before I was a Christian, my life was going nowhere.

I felt emptiness inside, and I wondered what was wrong, what was missing. One day, I went to a church service and heard the pastor say that we are all separated from God because of our sin. But because God loved us, He sent His Son to die in our place and bridge the gap between Him and us." Then, when you're finished, you can say something like, "Let me ask you, what do you think about that? Have you ever heard that before?" It's a way to share the gospel while telling your own story.

So what's your story? Everyone has one. Everyone has a testimony—and every testimony is valid. Granted, some are more dramatic than others.

We've heard of individuals who've been through horrific tragedies and survived to tell their stories. In some testimonies, the person used to be a gang member, a drug user, an alcoholic, or someone who served time in prison. His or her testimony is a great before-and-after story. Then there are those with less dramatic stories, such as the relatively moral, honest, hardworking person who realized a need for Jesus as well.

When you really get down to it, everyone's testimony is essentially the same:

We were all lost. We were all separated from God. We were all guilty, lonely, afraid to die, and on our way to hell. Then Jesus Christ, in His grace, intervened in our lives and transformed us. That is your story and mine—*and it's worth telling*.

So far, we've learned that Jesus addressed the words of the Great Commission to every one of His followers—not just to pastors, teachers, evangelists, or missionaries, but to any person anywhere who calls on the name of Christ. It is a command from our Lord to share the gospel. We've looked at the *who, where, why,* and *what* of evangelism. And we have learned what it means to be justified and sanctified.

Now let's look at a classic example of the power of a changed life. There is no better example of how to do evangelism than Jesus Christ Himself. He was the Master Communicator, the Master Evangelist. This is beautifully illustrated in the story of the woman at the well:

> He left Judea and departed again to Galilee. But He needed to go through Samaria.
>
> So He came to a city of Samaria which is called Sychar, near the plot of ground that Jacob gave to his son Joseph. Now Jacob's well was there. Jesus therefore, being wearied from His journey, sat thus by the well. It was about the sixth hour.
>
> A woman of Samaria came to draw water. Jesus said to her, "Give Me a drink." (John 4:3–7)

Verse 4 tells us that Jesus "needed to go through Samaria." A little historical background will help us understand the context. No orthodox Jew would ever travel to Galilee *through* Samaria, even though going through Samaria was a shortcut. Most Jews would not go through Samaria because of a deep-seated bigotry and prejudice. Samaritans hated Jews. Jews hated Samaritans.

Yet Jesus, a Jew and a rabbi, "needed to go through Samaria." Why? Well, because in Samaria, there was a burned-out, empty, searching, lonely woman who had an appointment with God. She expressed her sin through rampant immorality, among other things, bouncing from man to man, marriage to marriage. Yet Jesus Christ took time to talk with her.

This serves as a reminder that the love of God transcends the boundaries of race, economics, and sin.

Go Where People Are

The first thing we learn from Jesus' example is that we have to go to where people are. Often Christians try to isolate themselves from unbelievers. For some, the goal is to get through a day without any contact with non-Christians. As I've said before, God hasn't called us to isolate ourselves; He's called us to infiltrate culture. That is our mission field.

God wants us to reach out to our grumpy neighbor, our inquisitive coworker, and all those other people we see every day. Jesus did not say that the whole world should go to church. But He did say *that the church should go to the whole world.* We must invade our world with the gospel.

That's one of the reasons we try to do everything we can to reach people in unexpected ways at Harvest Ministries. In addition to our church services and Harvest Crusades, we reach out to people through the Internet, television, radio, and our podcasts.

People are searching. So we need to go where people are.

Use Tact

The second thing we learn is that when sharing the gospel we need to use tact. Tact is the intuitive knowledge that allows one to say the right thing at the right time. Jesus, the Master Evangelist, understood this.

However, I have seen believers sometimes approach non-Christians with really strange and even rude language. I have heard some say, "Hey, you sinner! Heathen Philistine! Come here for a second! Did you know that you are going to hell?" Afterward they will say, "Man, some people are just offended by the gospel!"

It's true that the gospel offends many people. There is indeed an offense in the truth. But sometimes people find offense because Christians can be weird, unnecessarily offensive, and don't know how to use tact. We need to bring a little winsomeness to the conversation and engage our listeners. We need to build a bridge to the person we are speaking with, such as finding some common interest. Arrest their attention. The idea is never to win the argument; *it's to win the soul.*

You might start a conversation, blasting them with your argument to the point that they never want to talk to a Christian again. That accomplishes nothing. What we want to do instead is to *try and win them over.*

Notice how Jesus tactfully and gracefully engaged the Samaritan woman: "Jesus answered, 'Everyone who drinks this water will be thirsty again, but whoever drinks the water I give him will never thirst. Indeed, the water I give him will become in him a spring of water welling up to eternal life'" (John 4:13–14 NIV). Jesus used the well and its water as a metaphor for her life.

The woman came to the well at the hottest part of the day because she was a social outcast. None of the other women would have anything to do with her because she'd been married and divorced five times and now lived with a sixth man. She was an immoral woman. So Jesus essentially said to her, "I understand what you are doing.

You are searching. You are trying to fill a void in your life with men and with sex, and it hasn't worked. And just as you can come to this well of water and not be satisfied, you can come to the well of relationships and pleasure and drink again and again, and you will never be satisfied. But if you drink from the water that I offer, you will never thirst."

So how did the woman respond? She flippantly shot back, "Sir, give me this water so that I won't get thirsty and have to keep coming here to draw water" (John 4:15 NIV).

Adapt to the Situation

This brings us to the third thing we see in Jesus' example as Master Evangelist: We must adapt to the situation.

This woman was accustomed to people being harsh with her. However, here was this Jewish man engaging her, *a Samaritan woman.* She probably braced herself for the insult, for the put-down. But there was no put-down from Jesus. It must have been hard for her to lower her defenses. She'd been chewed up and spit out by life, used and abused by men, and here was this man talking to her about living water. When she came back at Him with an edge of sarcasm in her voice, He identified the fact that she'd been living in sin. She claimed to have no husband, and Jesus used this opportunity to put His finger on that dark spot in her life: "Jesus said to her, 'You are right when you say you have no husband. The fact is, you have had five husbands, and the man you now have is not your husband. What you have just said is quite true'" (John 4:17–18 NIV).

As I pointed out earlier, people cannot fully appreciate the good news until they understand the bad news. When you talk to people about the Lord, they might ask whether they have to give up a certain lifestyle. Sometimes Christians are afraid to deal with that truth. But it is best to be honest and say, "Absolutely, you need to turn from that lifestyle, because it's a sin." That might offend the person, but it is the truth. Do it lovingly and do it with grace, but don't back off.

When the rich young ruler came to Jesus and said, "'Good teacher, what must I do to inherit eternal life?' ... [Jesus] said to him, 'You still lack one thing. Sell everything you have and give to the poor, and you will have treasure in heaven. Then come, follow me'" (Luke 18:18, 22 NIV). Jesus never said that to any other person, but He says it here and He doesn't pull any punches. He told the man to make a sacrifice to follow Him.

As Jesus engaged the woman at the well in dialogue, she became uncomfortable. He had turned a laser beam on her sin. So she tried to get Him off the subject: "Our fathers worshiped on this mountain, but you Jews claim that the place where we must worship is in Jerusalem" (John 4:20 NIV).

Jews and Samaritans had been debating about where God should be worshipped. The Jews believed that He was to be worshipped in Jerusalem, where the temple, priests, and sacrificial system were located. But the Samaritans had their own temple and their own views. Jesus could have jumped on this issue because it was a hotly debated topic of that day. Instead, He answered her question succinctly, pointing out what was right, bringing it back to the big issue: "God is spirit, and his worshipers must worship in spirit and in truth" (John 4:24 NIV).

People will try to send you off on a rabbit trail when you're sharing the gospel. When you start to get personal, talking of their need for God, they'll come back with comments like, "Well, wait. If God is so good, then why does He allow suffering? And what about people who have never heard about Jesus Christ? What will God do with them?"

As you answer one question, they'll move on to another. That is a diversionary tactic, sometimes employed when someone doesn't want to talk about himself or herself. When this happens, I simply try to answer the question to the best of my ability, and then bring the conversation back to the person's need for Jesus Christ.

This is exactly what Jesus did with the Samaritan woman. He brought her back to what really mattered, *what was essential.* As a result, her cynicism gave way to curiosity. She started to believe: "'I know that Messiah is coming' (who is called Christ). 'When He comes, He will tell us all things.' Jesus said to her, 'I who speak to you am He'" (John 4:25–26).

Tell Your Story

This brings us to the fourth thing we need to remember when we're sharing the gospel: Telling our story is a powerful bridge for the gospel message. We see that the Samaritan woman, minutes old as a believer, immediately went out and began to tell others:

> The woman then left her waterpot, went her way
> into the city, and said to the men, "Come, see a
> Man who told me all things that I ever did. Could
> this be the Christ?" Then they went out of the city
> and came to Him. (John 4:28–30)

There's great power in the simplicity of a changed life. This woman's testimony was so powerful that people believed in Jesus as a result. We read that "many of the Samaritans from that town believed in him because of the woman's testimony, 'He told me everything I ever did'" (John 4:39 NIV).

This was the power of a changed life.

That's why it's so important to share the before and after of what God did in your life. You may have such an amazing story that others find it difficult to believe you are the same person because your life was so transformed by Jesus Christ. Sharing about that transformation can speak to someone in a special way.

I find it interesting how often the apostle Paul, a brilliant orator, a great communicator, and a wonderful intellect, would use his testimony to speak to people. We see in Acts 24 that when he spoke before the Roman governor, he began with his own story. Then he moved to the core message of the gospel.

So what's the best way to tell your story? What should you include? What should you *not* include?

Don't Glorify or Exaggerate Your Past

First, don't glorify or exaggerate your past. Accuracy and truthfulness are important. I bring this up because some Christians' testimonies change with the passing of time, becoming more dramatic. Be totally honest and tell the truth.

Another problem is making your past sound more appealing than your present. I have heard believers share their testimonies about all the things they once did and they make the old days sound better than their new lives in Christ! It makes me wonder if they really understand what it means to be a Christian. Paul, in speaking of his past, said,

> I once thought these things were valuable, but now I consider them worthless because of what Christ has done. Yes, everything else is worthless when compared with the infinite value of knowing Christ Jesus my Lord. For his sake I have discarded everything else, counting it all as garbage, so that I could gain Christ. (Phil. 3:7–8 NLT)

The word *garbage* can also be translated as "dung." Paul was making a point. What word could be more offensive than that? When I walk my dog, I certainly don't enjoy cleaning up after him. The first thing I want to do is find the nearest trash receptacle. I don't save what my dog left behind, and I certainly don't brag about it to other people. I see it for what it is: *excrement, refuse.*

If you see your life before Christ as a wonderful thing, then you're not seeing it as it really was. Whatever you did then, you were heading for certain judgment, and God, in His grace, invaded your world and redeemed you. When you tell your story, instead of glorifying your past, glorify the Lord and talk about what He's done for you.

Remember, It's about Him

Second, when you tell your story, remember that it's not about you. It's about Him. Don't dwell too long on your story, because it is only a bridge—*a bridge to the big story of Jesus.* Make a beeline for the cross. That's the part of the story you want to get to: His love for humanity, His death, His resurrection from the dead, and how He transforms people's lives.

Be Patient

We must be patient in the work of sharing the gospel. I cannot emphasize enough that conversion is the work of God and God alone. He is looking for laborers in the field, and every one of us has an important part to play. Sometimes it is just planting a seed. At other times, it is watering a seed that someone else planted. And sometimes, by God's grace, it is reaping what others have planted and watered.

Following this line of thinking, Paul said,

> I planted the seed, Apollos watered it, but God made it grow. So neither he who plants nor he who waters is anything, but only God, who makes things grow. The man who plants and the man who waters have one purpose, and each will be rewarded according to his own labor. (1 Cor. 3:6–8 NIV)

Just be faithful in planting the seeds. Sometimes seed planting is sharing the entire gospel. At other times, it's telling a little of your story. Sometimes it's just saying to an unbeliever who is hurting, "I will remember to pray for you." Sometimes seed planting is as simple as being a good example.

Then again, you might be watering seeds planted by others. As you look back on your own conversion, you can probably recall the events that led to it. Certain things began to soften your heart, things that touched you and made you more open to the gospel. The seeds being planted in the lives of unbelievers today are likewise so important.

Maybe you get a little discouraged because you've been doing a lot of planting, but you haven't seen any results. Remember, though, that a farmer needs to be patient. Ecclesiastes 3:11 says, "Yet God has made everything beautiful for its own time. He has planted eternity in the human heart, but even so, people cannot see the whole scope of God's work from beginning to end" (NLT). We must be patient in planting seeds and in sharing the gospel and not give up. As Paul wrote to Timothy, "A servant of the Lord must not quarrel but must be kind to everyone, be able to teach, and be patient with difficult people" (2 Tim. 2:24 NLT).

The seeds you plant today may break ground tomorrow. That bit of truth you shared with someone might be like a time bomb that detonates later, because God says that His Word won't return void (Isa. 55:11). You see, the harvest doesn't happen at the end of a church service; the harvest happens at the end of the age. So we need to keep praying and believing that God will use His Word.

I've conducted funeral services for Christians who prayed for someone their entire lives, only to have that person come to Christ *at their funeral.* We never know when the seeds we've planted are going to break ground.

Many times we are tempted to think we haven't made a difference for the kingdom, like missionary George Smith, who thought his entire ministry was a failure. He'd been in Africa only a short time when he was driven out of the country. He left behind a Bible and one convert, a poor woman. Not long after that, George Smith died on his knees, praying for Africa.

A number of years later, a group of men stumbled into the place in Africa where George Smith had once ministered. They found the woman, who testified to them of her faith in Christ. *Then she led them to Christ.*

Afterward, those men went out and reached others in their area. And the ones they reached also reached others. One hundred years later, thousands of converts could be directly traced to the one woman Smith led to Christ so many years earlier.

Like George Smith, maybe you'll reach only one person in your entire life. But what if that person becomes another Billy Graham? Maybe you will reach only a handful of people and never see the fruit of it in your lifetime. It may not be until years after you've left this earth. But God will be faithful with His Word.

We are told in Galatians 6:9, "Let us not become weary in doing good, for at the proper time we will reap a harvest if we do not give up" (NIV).

So just be faithful.

Keep planting those seeds.

Keep praying for those who don't know Christ.

Keep looking for ways to build bridges to unbelievers.

Keep sharing your story of what God has done for you.

Three Keys to Sharing Your Story[1]

1. Your life before Christ. Don't glorify your past, but talk about how you were before Christ.

2. Your life changed by Christ. Summarize how you came into a relationship with Christ, and be sure to mention the key elements of the gospel.

3. Your new life in Christ. Talk about how your life is noticeably different now that you follow Christ. Put the following benefits of being in Christ in your own words: peace (Rom. 5:1), a purpose for living (Jer. 29:11), and the assurance that you're going to heaven (John 3:36).

19

SHARING THE GOSPEL EFFECTIVELY

Is there a right and wrong way to share the gospel of Jesus Christ? Are there certain essentials that must be in our presentation so that the gospel truly is the gospel? Is there a way to be more effective in doing this? The answer to all those questions is a resounding *yes!*

When our efforts at sharing aren't successful, we console ourselves with the words of Matthew 5:10: "Blessed are those who are persecuted because of righteousness, for theirs is the kingdom of heaven" (NIV). However, as I said before, we're often "persecuted" for being obnoxious, strange, or just plain weird. And far too often, the worst offenders are the ones who should be the greatest example: *preachers.* I have often wondered where many of the bizarre ministers we see on television come from. Do they talk that way all the time? People will look at these self-appointed representatives of the Christian faith and write off all Christians. If all I knew of Christianity was what I saw on some Christian shows today, I would think Christians were crazy too.

Many times, unbelievers aren't rejecting the gospel as much as they are rejecting the way it is presented.

Anticipating Attacks

The devil will always oppose the person God uses to share His truth. When Christians, motivated by love for non-Christians, reach out and invite others to heaven, the devil seeks to pull them down to hell. When the people of God say, "Let us rise up and build," the devil and his demons say, "Let us rise up and oppose." Don't let that terrify you, but let it educate you. Jesus said we are His church, and "the gates of Hades shall not prevail against it" (Matt. 16:18).

In Acts 14, we see two modes of attack often used by the enemy, both designed to stop the person God is using:

Outward attack: "The Jews who refused to believe stirred up the Gentiles and poisoned their minds against the brothers" (Acts 14:2 NIV); "Then some Jews came from Antioch and Iconium and won the crowd over. They stoned Paul and dragged him outside the city, thinking he was dead" (v. 19 NIV). The outward attacks on Paul came in the form of slander, threats, and actual physical harm.

Inward attack: "When the crowd saw what Paul had done, they shouted in the Lycaonian language, 'The gods have come down to us in human form!'" (v. 11 NIV). Paul's inward attack came in the form of worship from the people. Popularity is often more deadly than persecution. One begins to believe the praise and become inflated with pride. Inward attacks can also come in the form of insecurity.

When God first begins to use you, the devil might whisper in your ear, "You're not worthy to be used by God," or "You'll fail.

No one will listen to you." That's when you decide to ignore him, remembering that "God has chosen the foolish things of the world to put to shame the wise" (1 Cor. 1:27) and "the eyes of the LORD run to and fro throughout the whole earth, to show Himself strong on behalf of those whose heart is loyal to Him" (2 Chron. 16:9).

So the devil changes his tactic. He whispers, "You're so wonderful! No one prays like you do. You're so powerful when you speak!" This tactic is much easier to succumb to, because many times you don't even realize that it's happening. This was the Old Testament prophet Samson's problem. He thought he could handle anything. We think his main sin was immorality, but the sin of pride made him think he could do whatever he wanted with impunity.

Sin can make you do stupid things.

Peter was also brought down by the devil's tactic of pride. We know that he denied the Lord three times. But the pride that preceded his denial was the true sin. In the Upper Room, he had said to Jesus, "Even if all fall away on account of you, I never will" (Matt. 26:33 NIV).

The best way we can pray for God's people, as well as for ourselves, is to ask God to help us remain humble and usable.

How easily Paul could have compromised in this area and rationalized that he would first draw the people to himself, and then tell them about Jesus. But once that path is taken, so many compromises have to be made that no one will listen once we get there.

The Catfish in Your Tank

Paul, after his difficulties, laid it out plainly for the believers: "We must go through many hardships to enter the kingdom of God"

(Acts 14:22 NIV). Paul later wrote to Timothy, "Yes, and all who desire to live godly in Christ Jesus will suffer persecution" (2 Tim. 3:12).

In many ways, you could say we are like the cod shipped from the East Coast to the West Coast. By the time the fish arrived in the west, it was spoiled. The supplier tried freezing the fish, only to have it arrive mushy to the taste. They tried shipping the fish live, but they all arrived dead. So they tried sending them live once again, but with one difference: *They included catfish in the tanks.* Catfish are the mortal enemies of cod, and wouldn't you know it, the cod arrived alive and well, having spent the entire trip eluding the catfish. People who ate the fish said it was the best they'd ever tasted.

In the same way, God may put a catfish in your tank, so to speak, to keep you alive and well spiritually. Consider what Jesus said about this:

> If the world hates you, you know that it hated Me before it hated you. If you were of the world, the world would love its own. Yet because you are not of the world, but I chose you out of the world, therefore the world hates you. Remember the word that I said to you, "A servant is not greater than his master." If they persecuted Me, they will also persecute you. (John 15:18–20)

Whenever the devil sees a work of God beginning to flourish, he puts up a roadblock. It may be an unexpected delay or even someone among our ranks who opposes the work. Judas, after all, spoke against Mary's pouring perfume on the feet of Jesus, protesting, "Why wasn't this perfume sold and the money given to the poor? It was worth a year's wages" (John 12:5 NIV). It sounds noble, but Judas was the treasurer, and he skimmed from the moneybox.

Whenever you attempt to do something to reach an unbeliever with the gospel, you will face clear-cut, satanic opposition.

The Secret of the "So"

Thankfully, Paul never allowed persecution to deter him, but instead was a persistent and effective communicator of the gospel. Acts 14:1 tells us, "At Iconium Paul and Barnabas went as usual into the Jewish synagogue. There they spoke so effectively that a great number of Jews and Gentiles believed" (NIV). The word *so* in this verse arrests our attention and says to all preachers, teachers, and those called to declare the gospel that there is a way to speak so that people will believe.

We see from this verse that there's a right way and a wrong way to share the gospel. Some people, in the way they declare it, make it *bad news* instead of the *good news*.

Others want to make the gospel more acceptable, so they water it down and fail to declare the "whole counsel of God" (Acts 20:27). It's tempting to leave out things that are uncomfortable to say. But what would you think of a doctor who wouldn't deliver any bad news? I would think he was a bad doctor. If people are given the truth, then at least they can do something about it. *If not, they will die.* It's better to make someone uncomfortable *temporarily* than to send them to death *permanently.*

Still others will try to make the gospel so eloquent that they will unnecessarily complicate the message. Paul said, "And I, brethren, when I came to you, did not come with excellence of speech or of wisdom declaring to you the testimony of God" (1 Cor. 2:1) and "Christ did not send me to baptize, but to preach the gospel, not with wisdom of words, lest the cross of Christ should be made of no effect" (1 Cor. 1:17).

It is not your objective to impress your listener with your theological depth or intellectual prowess. Your objective is to speak in a way that they can understand so they can respond.

Here we discover the secret of the "so." In other words, the secret of an effectively shared gospel:

- It will be clear, simple, and focused on the work of Jesus Christ on the cross.
- It will be unapologetically biblical.
- It will be truthful, yet lovingly shared.

Paul continued preaching the gospel message, undeterred by the tremendous obstacles he encountered. He stands today as a great example of what it means to communicate the gospel clearly, intelligently, and without compromise.

May we do the same!

20

MAKING DISCIPLES

I'll let you in on a little secret: I've always feared preaching the gospel. I had to face that fear one day—and the time came sooner than I expected.

I was a young Christian and had planned to attend a baptism service down at Newport Beach. But when I arrived, the service was ending rather than beginning. Even so, a few Christians had stayed behind to hold an informal worship service on the beach. So I walked over to the little group and sat down. No one was leading the group. Someone would begin singing a worship song and everyone else would join in. I hadn't been there long when I felt a strong urge to share a Scripture passage I had read that morning.

"Uh, excuse me," I said as a song was ending. "I read a Scripture this morning that I would like to share." I nervously read through the passage and then talked a little about what God had shown me in those verses.

When I finished speaking, a young woman who had just walked up with her friend said, "Excuse me, Pastor. We missed the baptism, and we were wondering if you could still baptize us?"

I quickly explained that I wasn't a pastor and that I didn't know how to baptize anyone. Even so, I was sensing that God wanted me to help them. So pretty soon, we made our way down to the water.

Although I had been baptized at this very beach and watched the pastors do other baptisms, I'd never paid close attention to how it was done. So as best as I could remember, I imitated what I had seen and slowly lowered the young woman down into the water and up again.

Relieved to see her still breathing, I then baptized her friend. "I baptize you in the name of the Father, of the Son, and of the Holy Spirit," I said.

Before I knew it, a crowd had gathered on the beach to watch. I felt the urge to preach the gospel to them, and so I did to the best of my ability. When I was finished speaking, I gave an invitation for people to receive Christ. A few responded, and I baptized them as well!

That day was a turning point for me. I discovered what it was like to be used of God to bring people to Him. And I've never been the same. It was a sneak preview of things that came later in my life.

This experience isn't something that only happens to a chosen few. God can and will use us to lead others to Christ. I believe that He can use all believers to fulfill the Great Commission, given to every follower of Christ. The issue is not so much *ability* as *availability.* We must simply be willing.

Expect Excuses

But as you approach people and begin to share your faith, you will be hit with a barrage of so-called reasons why they don't want to come to Christ. I would suggest that they are excuses. Excuses speak of a lack of will. It has been said that "an excuse is the skin of a reason stuffed with a lie." It is something we say when we don't want to do something. George Washington said, "It is better to offer no excuse than a bad one."[1]

Jesus told the story of a king who invited his subjects to a great wedding feast for his son. "But they were not concerned and paid no attention [they ignored and made light of the summons, treating it with contempt] and they went away—one to his farm, another to his business" (Matt. 22:5 AB). In other words, they made excuses for not accepting the king's invitation.

In the same way, many people have a lot of bad excuses about why they will not give their lives to Jesus Christ. But there's really only one primary reason.

It's not because they struggle with the gospel philosophically or intellectually. The issue is not evolution or the legitimacy of the resurrection of Christ. It is not whether the Bible is "full of contradictions." And it's not about where Cain's wife came from. These explanations, for the most part, are all excuses, plain and simple.

There are exceptions of course. Some people with legitimate questions will have to recognize they're not going to get answers for every possible issue. Still, there are others who hide behind those questions, instead of wrestling with the unanswered mysteries of the faith.

This is why we must pray for discernment when we are sharing our faith. Scripture warns, "Do not give what is holy to the dogs; nor cast your pearls before swine, lest they trample them under their feet, and turn and tear you in pieces" (Matt. 7:6). Pigs don't appreciate pearls, just like my dog can't appreciate certain things. It would be a waste to take him to a movie or a concert. He's not interested in those things, and he is especially uninterested in my sermons. He actually attended Harvest Christian Fellowship before he became my family's dog. He had been in training as a guide dog for the blind, so his trainers brought him every Sunday. He would sit patiently and wait during the worship. But as soon as my message ran past thirty minutes, he would start to groan audibly in the service.

So when we're sharing with an unbeliever and all we get is mockery, argument, and rejection, we might want to terminate the conversation. Then again, if God leads us to continue, we should continue.

In Scripture, there were times when Jesus wouldn't even reveal truth to some people. He never spoke a single word to King Herod, who wanted to see a miracle from Him. *Why?* Herod was not a true seeker. John 2:23–24 offers this additional insight about why Jesus didn't engage certain individuals: "Now when He was in Jerusalem at the Passover, during the feast, many believed in His name when they saw the signs which He did. But Jesus did not commit Himself to them, because He knew all men." Think of all those potential converts. But Jesus knew their hearts.

God said He would reveal Himself to the true seeker (Jer. 29:13). If people genuinely seek the truth, they will find their way to Jesus Christ. And Jesus Christ will find His way to them.

By the same token, if people are *not* genuine seekers of the truth, that will become evident by the excuses they make, and Jesus won't bother.

Many will insist that teaching Jesus Christ is the only way to God is narrow, insensitive, and intolerant. Amazingly, this issue has become controversial even in modern times. A 1997 article in the *Los Angeles Times* reported on a two-day seminar to promote a "theology of pluralism" that opposes the teaching that Jesus Christ is the only way to God.

Rev. Ronald F. Thiemann, former dean of the Divinity School of Harvard University, was quoted as saying, "There might be [non-Christian] companions with us who also witness to God's truth." He said that, for the sake of the gospel, Christians need to be open to the Spirit's leading.[2] No, for the sake of the gospel, Christians must proclaim the truth according to Scripture. The Spirit's leading will always confirm what is written in the Bible. The Bible is the blueprint we must follow.

Saying that Jesus Christ is the only way to the Father is a bedrock issue of the Christian faith. There can be no compromise here. Again, as Paul wrote to the believers in Galatia:

> I am astonished that you are so quickly deserting the one who called you by the grace of Christ and are turning to a different gospel—which is really no gospel at all. Evidently some people are throwing you into confusion and are trying to pervert the gospel of Christ. But even if we or an angel from heaven should preach a gospel other than the one we preached to you, let him be eternally condemned! (Gal. 1:6–8 NIV)

It's an either/or proposition. If we declare anything less than the truth, we are preaching a false gospel. People may want to believe that all roads lead to God. They may sincerely hope that every religion is basically true and that they somehow all blend together beautifully. *But they don't.*

Where Beliefs Collide

For example, Buddhists deny the existence of a personal God. Hindus believe that God is formless and abstract, taking both the form of a trinity and the forms of millions of lesser gods. In direct contrast, the Bible teaches that God is a personal deity who created us in His own image, loves us, and wants to have a relationship with us.

Buddhists believe salvation comes through self-effort alone, with no personal God to help or guide you. Hindus believe devotion, works, and self-control can achieve salvation. Muslims insist that man pays for his own sins, earns his own salvation, and can never be certain whether he has achieved salvation. In stark contrast, the Bible teaches that Jesus Christ died for our sins. The Bible says that salvation is a free gift, apart from works, given to us by a personal God. It also teaches that we can have absolute assurance of going to heaven when we die.

Concerning Jesus Christ, Buddhists believe that He was a good teacher, but less important than Buddha himself. Hindus believe that Jesus was just one of many incarnations, or sons, of God. They teach that Christ was not the one and only Son of God, that He was no more divine than any other man, and that He did not die for our sins. Muslims will tell you that Jesus Christ was only a man—a prophet equal to Adam, Noah, or Abraham, all of whom are below Muhammad in importance in the Muslim faith. The Qur'an teaches that Christ did not die for the sins of humanity, but that Judas, not

Jesus, died on the cross. Muslims believe that Judas was mistaken for Jesus, and that Christ lived a long life. They also reject the preexistence of Jesus and His death and resurrection.

In direct contrast, the Bible teaches that Jesus Christ was God in human form and that He was the one and only Son of God. The Bible tell us that Jesus was and is the Savior of the world who died and rose again and who will personally come into the heart of and transform anyone who calls on Him.

So you see, it doesn't work to believe *all of the above*. The tenets of these extremely diverse religions directly contradict one another. They simply cannot all be true. Buddhists, Muslims, and Hindus have no assurance they will get to heaven. Only Christianity holds that wonderful, life-transforming hope!

Pop the Question!

After answering the questions of non-Christians, what do you do next? Now is the time to close the deal, so to speak. Maybe the reason that many of us have never led another person to Christ is because we've never "popped the question."

I never officially popped the question with my wife, Cathe. Rather than getting down on one knee and proposing, I said, "Well, I guess we're going to get married!" Cathe wasn't even sure I had proposed until later. Somehow we decided to get married, but Cathe doesn't remember a formal, official proposal on my part and neither do I.

So it's important for us to ask people, "Would you like to ask Jesus Christ into your life right now?" It isn't necessary to pressure someone, but we should simply and prayerfully ask.

The No Answer

The answer might be "I don't feel ready yet." That's a good time to ask why, and if you can help in any way. The answer still might be no, but you can explain how they can pray later, if they choose to. You can add, "I am confident that God will respond, because He said, 'You will seek Me and find Me, when you search for Me with all your heart'" (Jer. 29:13).

The Yes Answer

The answer also might be yes. So go ahead and pray with the person at that moment. What a joy it is to pray with someone to make this commitment or to bring a person to church or a crusade and see him or her walk forward at the invitation! The Bible says there is joy in heaven over one sinner who comes to repentance (Luke 15:7).

Start Discipling

So once you've prayed with someone to make a commitment to Christ, is that the end of it? *No.* That's the beginning. Now it is your privilege—*and your responsibility*—to disciple this person. Going back to the Great Commission, we are commanded to "go therefore and *make disciples of all the nations,* baptizing them in the name of the Father and of the Son and of the Holy Spirit, *teaching them* to observe all things that I have commanded you" (Matt. 28:19–20). We often emphasize the "go" of this verse, only to overlook making disciples and teaching them.

We are first to be disciples of Jesus Christ, and then we are called to repeat the process. "So we tell others about Christ, warning every-one and teaching everyone with all the wisdom God has given us. We want to present them to God, perfect in their relationship to Christ" (Col. 1:28 NLT). Paul wrote to Timothy, "You have heard me teach things that have been confirmed by many reliable witnesses. Now teach these truths to other trustworthy people who will be able to pass them on to others" (2 Tim. 2:2 NLT).

I am so thankful that someone did this for me. After I accepted Christ during that lunch hour on my high school campus, no one gave me a Bible or prayed with me afterward. I was on my own. So the next weekend, I went off to the woods to do drugs. But God spoke to my heart that weekend and told me, "You don't need that anymore."

The following Monday, a Christian named Mark walked up to me at school and said, "Hi, I saw you at the Bible study, and I noticed you went forward and accepted Christ."

"Yeah," I responded defensively.

"Well," he said. "I am a Christian, and I want to help you get strong spiritually. Do you have a Bible?"

"No, I don't have one yet."

Mark gave me a Bible and invited me to go to church with him. He drove me to church, where he introduced me to other Christians. He invited me over to his house, where I met his parents, who were also Christians. Mark and his family patiently answered my questions and showed me what it was like to be a Christian in the real world, which I desperately needed. I was able to *see* how to live the Christian life.

You may not consider yourself a biblical scholar, but you can still play a key role in the life of a new believer. For many new Christians, the problem is acclimating to the Christian life. They need teaching but they also need a personal example. In short, they need a friend.

Later in his life, Paul mentored young Timothy. "But you, Timothy, certainly know what I teach, and how I live, and what my purpose in life is. You know my faith, my patience, my love, and my endurance" (2 Tim. 3:10 NLT). That kind of personal knowledge comes from spending time with someone. And Paul wrote to the church at Thessalonica, "For you know that we dealt with each of you as a father deals with his own children, encouraging, comforting and urging you to live lives worthy of God, who calls you into his kingdom and glory" (1 Thess. 2:11–12 NIV).

Not only does discipleship benefit new believers, it also benefits us. You see, after we've been Christians for a time, we need an outlet for what we're learning. God hasn't given us the privilege of hearing His Word so we can become sermon connoisseurs. We are to take what He gave us and share it with others. I am firmly convinced that to maintain input without output is hazardous to our spiritual growth and progress. We as believers can be in serious danger if, in our attendance of Bible studies, prayer meetings, and intake of spiritual information, we do not have an adequate outlet for these newfound truths. In our evangelizing and mentoring of others, we not only save sinners from hell, but we also save ourselves from spiritual stagnation.

If you take a new believer under your wing, it could bring revival to your life. Whether it's leading a person to Christ or discipling someone who has just accepted Him, you need the outlet as much as he or she needs the input. New believers need our wisdom, knowledge, and experience as mature believers. And we as mature believers need their childlike simplicity of faith, their zeal, and their first-love relationship with Jesus.

It's like going to Disneyland with adults versus going there with children. When you go to Disneyland with adults, what do you want to do first (after complaining about how expensive it is)? You want to eat! But after you eat, you're not ready to go on any rides—you're ready to take a nap. You get in line anyway and then complain about the long wait.

But when you go to Disneyland with children, it's a different experience altogether. It's all so real through their eyes. I remember when I first took my sons there. I loved pointing out Sleeping Beauty's castle and watching their expressions when they spotted Mickey Mouse walking down the street. When you look at something through the eyes of a child, it becomes a whole new experience.

Taking a new believer under your wing and seeing life the way he or she sees it can bring back things you have forgotten. It will rekindle your fire. That's why you need to do everything you can to try to bring people to Christ and find someone new in the faith and offer to help them grow spiritually. The Bible says, "A generous man will prosper; he who refreshes others will himself be refreshed" (Prov. 11:25 NIV).

Maybe God will never call you to be a pastor or a missionary. But what if you answered God's call to disciple someone He brought into your life and that person went on to change the world? You would have the joy of knowing that you played an important role in this person's life. As Daniel 12:3 says, "Those who are wise shall shine like the brightness of the firmament, and those who turn many to righteousness like the stars forever and ever."

God wants to use you to fulfill His Great Commission. Let's pray that the Lord will use us in these critical times in which we live. Even today, the harvest is great but the laborers are few!

NOTES

Introduction

1. Ray C. Stedman, "The Coming of Joy" (sermon, Peninsula Bible Church, Palo Alto, CA, December 19, 1976), www.pbc.org/files/messages/11623/3018.html.

Chapter 1: God's Cure for Heart Trouble

1. John W. Newcomer, et al., "Decreased Memory Performance in Healthy Humans Induced by Stress-Level Cortisol Treatment," *Arch Gen Psychiatry* 56, no. 6 (1999): 527–533.

2. Associated Press, "Poll: Americans worry about nuclear weapons," *MSNBC,* March 30, 2005, www.msnbc.msn.com/id/7340591/from/RL.3//.

3. Ibid.

4. Jeffrey Kluger, et al., "Fear Not!" *Time,* April 2, 2001, www.time.com/time/magazine/article/0,9171,999584-1,00.html.

5. C. S. Lewis, *The Problem of Pain* (San Francisco: HarperCollins, 2001), 149.

6. "General Douglas MacArthur's Leyte Landing—'I Have Returned,'" *All Philippines,* October 20, 2009, www.allphilippines.com/?p=567.

Chapter 2: Everyday Jesus

1. Brian McCollum, *Detroit Free Press,* June 30, 2000, www.eminem4ever.eminemforum.com/flashed/info/interviews/interview13.html.

2. *Teen Vogue,* June/July 2004, 83.

3. Austin Scaggs, "The Devil and Dave Matthews," *Rolling Stone,* January 22, 2004, http://dbtp.squarespace.com/newsarticles/2004/1/23/the-devil-and-dave-matthews.html.

4. "Trouble Lyrics," Sing 365.com, accessed December 20, 2005, www.sing365.com/music/lyric.nsf/Trouble-lyrics-Dave-Matthews-Band-and-DaveMatthews/ED6C178F4706E8E048256DAB0029FD7D.

Chapter 3: Famous Last Words

1. Voltaire, quoted in *The Evidence Bible,* comp. Ray Comfort (Alachua, FL: Bridge-Logos, 2003), 1504.

2. Voltaire, quoted in Daniel Barclay Williams, *Freedom and Progress* (Petersburg, VA: 1890), 111.

3. *Most,* directed by Bobby Garabedian, Eastwind Films, Prague Indies Productions, 2003.

Chapter 4: How to Change Your Life

1. "12-Step Son," *People,* May 12, 2003, www.people.com/people/archive/article/0,,20140023,00.html.

Chapter 6: Are You His Disciple?

1. William Booth, quoted in Cristina E. Rodríguez, *Soul Survival* (Fairfax, VA: Xulon Press, 2003), 77.

2. Samuel Rutherford, quoted in *The Christian Pioneer*, ed. J. F. Winks, vol. 20, (London: 1886), 24.

3. J. Dwight Pentecost, *Design for Discipleship* (Grand Rapids, MI: Kregel, 1996).

Chapter 9: Discipleship and the Bible

1. Abraham Lincoln, *The Lincoln Yearbook*, comp. J. T. Hobson (Dayton, OH: United Brethren, 1912), 197.

Chapter 10: Discipleship and Prayer

1. Martin Luther, *The Place of Trust: Martin Luther on the Sermon on the Mount*, ed. Martin E. Marty (New York: Harper & Row, 1983), 34.

Chapter 14: First-Century Principles for Reaching the Twenty-First Century

1. Billy Graham, *Just As I Am: The Autobiography of Billy Graham* (San Francisco: HarperCollins, 1999), 565.

2. C. H. Spurgeon, *Metropolitan Tabernacle Pulpit* (Pasadena, TX: Pilgrim, 1971), 22:143–144.

3. C. H. Spurgeon, *The Autobiography* (Cincinnati: 1899), 3:63.

4. D. L. Moody, *Secret Power* (Chicago: 1881), 72.

Chapter 15: The Three *W*s of Evangelism

1. Campus Crusade for Christ, *The Four Spiritual Laws* (Orlando: New Life Publications, 1965, 1968), www.campuscrusade.com/fourlawseng.htm.

2. Tip O'Neill, Jr., *Man of the House,* with William Novak (New York: Random, 1987), 39.

3. Charles Peace, quoted in *The Princeton Seminary Bulletin* 4, no. 1, (1910): 9.

4. Billy Graham, "The Evangelist and His Preaching: We Set Forth the Truth Plainly" in *The Work of an Evangelist* (Minneapolis, MN: World Wide, 1984), www.preaching.com/sermons/11566810/page-2/.

5. Blaise Pascal, *Pensees,* trans. A. J. Krailsheimer (London: Penguin, 1993), 45.

6. D. L. Moody, quoted in James K. Wellman Jr., *The Gold Coast Church and the Ghetto* (Urbana: University of Illinois, 1999), 111.

Chapter 16: The "What" of Evangelism: The Gospel

1. Doug Fletcher, "Mt Everest 2006: Sometimes, Who Lives and Who Dies Depends on Who Cares," EverestNews.com, June 25, 2006, www.everestnews.com/2006expeditions/everest006252006.htm.

2. Allen G. Breed and Binaj Gurubacharya, "Everest Remains Deadly Draw for Climbers," USAToday.com, July 16, 2006, www.usatoday.com/tech/science/2006-07-16-everest-david-sharp_x.htm.

3. C. S. Lewis, *Mere Christianity,* rev. ed. (San Francisco: HarperCollins, 2001), 155.

4. Ray Recchi, "One Bad Apple Spoils It For The Whole Bunch," *SunSentinel,* May 28, 1992, http://articles.sun-sentinel.com/1992-05-28/features/9202110555_1_bad-checks-fred-turner-gas-stations.

5. *The Last Emperor,* directed by Bernardo Bertolucci (Recorded Picture Company, Hemdale Film, Yanco Films Limited, 1987).

6. C. H. Spurgeon, quoted in Robert Tarbell Oliver, *Public Speaking in the Reshaping of Great Britain* (Cranbury, NJ: Associated University, 1987), 105.

Chapter 17: Practical Effects of Salvation

1. C. H. Spurgeon, *Spurgeon at His Best,* comp. Tom Carter (Grand Rapids, MI: Baker, 1988), 116.

2. Corrie ten Boom, quoted in Carole C. Carlson, *Corrie ten Boom: Her Life, Her Faith* (New York: Jove, 1984), 141.

3. William R. Moody, *The Life of D. L. Moody* (Murfreesboro, TN: Sword of the Lord Publishers, 1980), 444.

4. Donald Grey Barnhouse, *Romans* (Grand Rapids, MI: Eerdmans, 1961), 2:12, quoted in John MacArthur, *The MacArthur New Testament Commentary,* vol. 20, *Romans 1–8* (Chicago: Moody, 1991), 318.

Chapter 18: What's Your Story?

1. Adapted from Greg Laurie, *How to Share Your One-Minute Message* (Riverside, CA: Harvest, 2003).

Chapter 20: Making Disciples

1. George Washington, quoted in *The Quotable Founding Fathers,* ed. Buckner F. Melton Jr. (Washington, DC: Brassey's, 2004), 81.

2. Larry B. Stammer, "No Religion Has a Monopoly on God's Truth, Clerics Assert," *The Los Angeles Times,* February 1, 1997, http://articles.latimes.com/1997-02-01/local/me-24465_1.

BIBLE RESOURCES